265

The Author

Rousas J. Rushdoony, editor of the *Philosophical and Historical Studies* series in the International Library of Philosophy and Theology, is an American writer and scholar. An ordained minister in the Orthodox Presbyterian Church, he has been a missionary among Paiute and Indians as well as pastor of two churches. Currently he lectures and is engaged in research. A to many theological and ph journals, Mr. Rushdoony is the *By What Standard?*, *Van Til* and *Freud* (Modern Thinkers Series), *Intellectual Schizophrenia,* and *The Messianic Character of American Education.*

THE NATURE
of the
AMERICAN SYSTEM

By

ROUSAS JOHN RUSHDOONY

The Craig Press
Nutley, New Jersey

Library of Congress Catalog Card Number: 64-7843

Printed in the United States of America

24470

To

Dr. Cornelius Van Til

Philosopher and Teacher

to the Generations

TABLE OF CONTENTS

iv

A PREFACE ON THE WRITING OF HISTORY

Revisionism is long overdue in American history, and in historical studies generally, lest history as a discipline disappears into the abysses of the social sciences. Ostensibly having arrived to new maturity in the hands of some practitioners as a science, history is rather becoming a fertile area of myth-making and quackery because it lacks any awareness of epistemological self-consciousness. It is assumed, first, that an objective history is possible, and also a valid science of history, and, second, it is assumed that if no objective history is possible, then history as a discipline is destroyed or else is reduced to propaganda.

Both assumptions must be rejected. Behind the writing of history is a philosophy of history, and behind that philosophy of history are certain pre-theoretical and essentially religious presuppositions. There is no such thing as brute factuality, but rather only interpreted factuality. The historian's report is always the report of a perspective, a context, a framework; man is not, like God, beyond time and circumstance, condition and place. Man is neither a prime mover nor a prime viewer, but, to deny to man the status of a first cause and a first view is by no means to deny the validity or function of secondary causes and secondary viewers. To recognize that man is neither a first cause nor a first viewer is thus to deny the possibility of an objective history, but it is not thereby a denial of the possibility of a valid history, unless we proceed on the assumption that the ordination and determination of first causes does violence to secondary causes and removes the liberty or contingency of second causes rather than establishing them. It is the insistence of orthodox Christian thought that the validity of history is pre-

v

cisely in its secondary status, and man's liberty is grounded on ultimate and transcendental order rather than on the myth of his own autonomy and ultimacy.

The writing of history then, because man is neither autonomous, objective or ultimately creative, is always in terms of a framework, a philosophical and ultimately religious framework in the mind of the historian. Thus, in U. S. history, we are told that certain data constitute the true history of the United States because they point to the conditions in the present which constitute the true moment of history. If Jesus be the Christ, the Messiah of history, then Abraham, Moses, David and John the Baptist are His forerunners; if Jesus is not the Christ, then the significance of these men recedes. If our philosophy be Marxist, then certain men and movements become the forerunners of the moment of truth. If we hold to the Liberal or Fabian Establishment, then clearly all preceding history must point forward to this blinding light, or be seen in reference to it. For earlier historians of this era, the light of Reason was this key to history. All of these historiographies have their incarnation, towards which they strive, or in terms of which they move, and present judgments as well as their Last Judgments are in terms of this incarnation. There is no neutralism. To assume neutralism is to assume the equal validity of all data, for their relative significance cannot be assessed until history is finished, all the reports in, and the consequent conclusions of the clash of data made apparent, if indeed conclusions are possible in a bland and meaningless world.

To the orthodox Christian, the shabby incarnations of the reigning historiographies are both absurd and offensive. They are idols, and he is forbidden to bow down to them and must indeed wage war against them. A Christian historiography and a Christian revisionism are thus for him moral imperatives.

For Christian revisionism, there is thus an incarnation as a central point in history, Jesus Christ, and, as Chalcedon clearly stated, this incarnation was without confusion of the eternal and the temporal, the divine and the human. This requires a denial of any coming, continuing, or possible incarnation in any historical order or institution. The divinization of church, state, school or any other institution, or

vi

its absorption into the incarnation, is thus a sign of paganism. Man and his institutions are truly temporal and historical; they can move to epistemological self-consciousness but never into the incarnation. The great gulf which separates strictly Christian historiography from all heresies, humanism, and paganism is this denial of the confusion, even in the unique incarnation of Jesus Christ, of the temporal and the eternal, the human and the divine. All other historiographies posit not only the possibility of an incarnated order of this confused sort but the absorption of all history into that order. It is held that autonomous man, as the historical ultimate, will both create that great historical moment, that incarnation of history, and will arrest and absorb history into that self-created eternity. Gnosticism is thus the end result of all heresies, and of Voegelin himself, for any hope in "the leap in being" is a hope in ultimate incarnation.

These essays are studies in Christian revisionism. Their purpose is to call attention to those aspects of American history currently neglected, namely, the Christian foundations which still militate against the present Gnostic and messianic movements. As noted in *This Independent Republic,* John Cotton was instrumental in giving to this country an anti-universalist and anti-perfectionist character. The promise of a "good" state was to him "the smell of a Leopard," of the beast, for the state was not the order of man's salvation. For Cotton, moreover, both liberty and power had to be limited, for man, as a secondary cause, could not claim the primary and total liberty and power of God. Against these premises war is being currently waged. The nature and history of that warfare in American history is the subject of these studies.

Rousas John Rushdoony
January 15, 1965.

CHAPTER I

THE NATURE OF THE AMERICAN SYSTEM

Periodically, there are protests over the use of the name *America* as a synonym for the United States, and *American* as the name of United States citizens. There is a measure of justice to this, in that the peoples of the North, South, and Central Americas are equally American, but, as understood by countless millions the world over, and by generations of immigrants, America means the United States, and America is the New World. The other countries are seen as derivative in culture and tradition: Spanish, British, Portuguese, or French, but America represents a fresh departure in history. Not only foreigners and immigrants, but Americans themselves have so read their history. This was, as Abraham Lincoln stated it in his Gettysburg address, "a new nation," a new proposition in history. George Washington, in his Farewell Address, saw that new nation as one not only with deep roots in the past, but one with an obligation to separate itself from dead Europe. "Our own" was to him something more than an eight year history, and "Europe" spelled to him a cycle of frustration. Therefore, "Why quit our own to stand upon foreign ground? Why, by interweaving our destiny with that of any part of Europe endanger our peace and prosperity in the toils of European Ambition, Rivalship, Interest, Humor or Caprice?" "Our destiny" was a very real thing to Washington, and it did not mean a return to Europe's present evil. Thomas Jefferson stated it very bluntly: "We are *maniacs* if we try to make Europe *moral* or to settle their disputes by *war.*"

Coupled with this sense of *newness and destiny* was a sense of *restoration.* The "ancient rights of freeborn Englishmen" and the "liberties of the Christian Church" were the central aspects of the American restoration.

To understand the nature of the American system, it is necessary to understand what it was that the colonists and constitutionalists were bent on restoring and furthering, and what the main causes of the American Revolution were. It should be noted in passing that the American Revolution was not a *revolution* in the modern sense of that word. After the French Revolution, that word gained a new connotation, one by no means applicable to the American event.

Two causes stand out clearly as basic to the break between the colonies and George III. The first cause was the religious issue. John Adams cited the attempt of parliament to force the establishment of the Church of England on the colonies as responsible, "as much as any other cause," for the break. "The objection was not merely to the office of a bishop, though even that was dreaded, but to the authority of parliament, on which it must be founded."[1] We can agree with Bridenbaugh that "It is indeed high time that we repossess the important historical truth that religion was a fundamental cause of the American Revolution."[2]   Every colony had its own form of Christian establishment or settlement; every one was a particular kind of Christian republic. It was to them a monstrous idea, to Anglicans as well as to Congregationalists and Presbyterians, for an alien body, Parliament, to impose an establishment upon them. The colonies were by nature and history *Christian*. Not only the religious settlements of New England and the central states, but the Southern colonies as well had their specifically Christian purpose and character. The word "plantation" in those days, whether applied to a New England or a southern settlement, had reference to a *religious* establishment of peoples. The concept of a secular state was virtually *non*-existent in 1776 as well as in 1787, when the Constitution was written, and no less so when the Bill of Rights was adopted. To read the Constitution as the charter for a secular state is to misread history, and to misread it radically. The Constitution was designed to *perpetuate* a Christian order.

---

[1] John Adams: *Works*, X, p. 185 (1865 edition), letter to Dr. Jedidiah Morse, 2 December, 1815.

[2] Carl Bridenbaugh: *Mitre and Sceptre*, Transatlantic Faiths, Ideas, Personalities and Politics, 1689-1775, p. xiv. New York: Oxford, 1962.

Let us consider the obvious rebuttal to such a statement, for it needs to be met: Why then is there, in the main, an *absence* of any reference to Christianity in the Constitution? The response must be equally blunt: There is an absence of reference because the framers of the Constitution did not believe that this was an area of jurisdiction for the federal government. It would not have occurred to them to attempt to re-establish that which the colonists had fought against, namely, religious control and establishment by the central government. The colonists would not have tolerated power in the Federal Union which they had rebelled against when claimed by crown and parliament. *Every* constituent state had some form of Christian establishment or settlement which it jealously guarded. This was an area of *states'* rights, not of federal control. The Constitution, by its doctrine of express powers, had barred the federal government from any jurisdiction over the churches by omission of reference to them in the grants of powers. Nonetheless, many clergymen as well as others were fearful and demanded a bill of rights and the specific exclusion from religion of the federal government.[3]

The First Amendment answered this demand: "Congress shall make no laws respecting an establishment of religion, or prohibiting the free exercise thereof." It should be noted, first, that nothing is here said about the separation of church and state. No such separation of Christianity, or church, and the state existed anywhere in the United States before, and, for some generations, after the ratification of this amendment. Second, the federal government did not secularize itself. Congress, both before and after ratification, began its sessions with divine worship and felt no inhibition in exercising its faith. Moreover, by re-enacting the Northwest Ordinance of July 13, 1787, *after* the adoption of the First Amendment, the federal government continued the policy of Article III: "Religion, morality, and knowledge being necessary to good government and the happiness of mankind, schools and the means of education shall forever be encouraged." To ensure the Christian order of the potential states, the territories were to be helped in this respect. Third, the rights of the constituent states to have their Christian order

[3] See Robert Allen Rutland: *The Birth of the Bill of Rights, 1776-1791*, pp. 127f., 151, 166. Chapel Hill: University of North Carolina Press, 1955.

without interference was underscored by barring *Congress,* i.e., the federal government, from either establishing or prohibiting religion. What the thirteen Christian republics had fought to maintain against crown and parliament they refused to surrender to a federal government. The freedom of the first amendment from federal interference is not *from* religion but *for* religion in the constituent states.

The establishments and settlements in the constituent states were definitely and specifically Christian. In most states, single or plural establishment prevailed. Where no church was established, Christianity as such was nonetheless firmly established. There were religious requirements for citizenship and suffrage, religious oaths, laws prohibiting blasphemy, laws requiring a trinitarian faith, or a firm belief in the infallibility of Scripture, and laws barring unbelievers as witnesses in court. Court decisions sometimes cited biblical law where civil law did not entirely fit the case.[4] In many areas, laws against unbelief were on the statute books. A man could be imprisoned for atheism. Warren Chase complained of it as an example of "slavery" and "barbarism" that in the 1820's "an old man was imprisoned sixty days, in Boston, for publishing in his own paper the fact that he did not believe in their orthodox God."[5] The laws were premised on the fact that the respective states were Christian, and anti-Christianity constituted treasonable activity or belief. The basis of the state being Christian, that foundation had to be protected legally. Although the U. S. Supreme Court is currently striking at some of these laws, many still remain on the books. The claim of the U. S. Supreme Court to jurisdiction in these affairs is a violation of the First Amendment, and has no real warrant in the Fourteenth Amendment. By claiming the right to intervene to disestablish, the U. S. Supreme Court has also implicitly established the power denied to it by the Constitution to prohibit religion. And, if the current move in the courts to compel taxation of

---

[4] For an example of this, an 1836 New Hampshire divorce case, see J. W. Ehrlich: *The Holy Bible and the Law,* pp. 64-69.   New York Oceana, 1962.

[5] *The Life-Line of the Lone One; or, Autobiography of Warren Chase (The World's Child),* p. 23, Boston: Colby and Rich, 1881, seventh edition.

the churches succeeds, it will place religion under state regulation.

The states, it has been noted, had their independent existence as Christian republics prior to the Revolution. They retained their prerogative here without diminution, sharing *none* of it with the federal government. They did, however, in varying degrees, share that prerogative with their constituent units, *the counties*. The counties, very often, adapted the law to their specific requirements. The reason for this was an obvious one: America represented a series of settlements by religious and ethnic groups, so that each area had and has its specific religious and ethnic orientation. According to a study of the current scene published in 1962, "in approximately one-half of the counties of the nation, a single religious body accounts for at least 50% of all the membership in the county."[6] The likelihood is that this is even more true of ethnic orientation, i.e., that most counties are dominated by a particular ethnic group. As one travels across the United States, the pluralistic character is readily apparent: one area will be Swedish and Lutheran, Mission Covenant and Evangelical Free Church; another county will be German and Roman Catholic, and Reformed; another Dutch, and Reformed Church and Christian Reformed; English and Episcopalian; Scotch-Irish and Presbyterian, and so on. As a result, until recently it was not uncommon to find nuns teaching in schools in one area, and the local Lutheran pastor dominant in his influence over the school in another area. In some areas, American born Germans speak English with an accent, and in other areas similar examples of the dominance of a local culture are apparent. America was *colonized* by various groups who congregated in sections of cities and specific rural areas *out of choice*. This fact re-enforced the basic localism of the American civil structure.

The second cause of the American Revolution was again a defense against invasion, an invasion of colonial self-government by parliament. The Revolution was actually a defensive war waged by the colonists against parliamentary troops.

To understand the significance of that invasion, it is necessary to recognize that the American civil structure was,

---

[6] Edwin Scott Gaustad: *Historical Atlas of Religion in America*, p. 159. New York: Harper and Row, 1962.

almost from its inception, *a Protestant restoration of feudal-ism.*[7]   To the colonists, as to the barons who wrested Magna Carta from King John, English liberty meant feudalism in essence, *localism as against centralism, contractual govern-ment as against absolutism.*   Almost at once, the colonies gravitated to localism and contractualism.   Their charters with the English crown were *feudal contracts,* and there was no relationship between colonies and crown except in terms of these charters.   Although the crown was often arbitrary, and sought to be absolutistic, the legal basis remained *feudal.*[8] Each colony was thus an independent state, with its own independent civil structure, under a feudal lord, represented in the colony by the royal governor.

In the colonies, this Protestant feudal restoration was steadily developed, even as absolutism was steadily developed in England.   At first, the crown claimed divine rights, and then, in 1688, parliament claimed the right to exercise royal absolutism in the name of the king.   On the other hand, in the colonies, and at times with astonishing rapidity, power gravitated from the state (i.e., the colony) to the local level. A large degree of *autonomy* was accorded to each town in Massachusetts as early as the General Court of 1635 because of the steady insistence on local self-government.[9]   Local of-ficers became locally elected.   In the declining days of feudal-ism in England, Robin Hood's enemy had been the sheriff and the county officials, all crown appointed; against these his feudal rebellion was directed.   Now, in America's feudal restoration, these officers were steadily made the county's men.   Any attempt, as that in Massachusetts to have the pay of judges taken over by the central authority in London, was bitterly resisted as an invasion of liberty.

Parliament, however, was bent on extending its power into the colonies, and the crown was agreeable to this en-

---

[7] See R. J. Rushdoony: *This Independent Republic.* Craig Press, Nutley, N. J., 1964.

[8] See Charles Howard McIlwain: *The American Revolution: A Constitutional Interpretation.*   Ithaca: Great Seal Bks, Cornell, (1923), 1961)

[9] See Sumner Chilton Powell: *Puritan Village, the Formation of a New England Town.*   Middletown, Conn.:   Wesleyan University Press, 1963; Thomas Jefferson Wertenbaker *The Puritan Oligarchy, The Founding of American Civilization,* p. 44f.: "Localism in Religion" went hand in hand with "localism in government."

croachment. Parliament, nonetheless, had no legal jurisdiction and its legislation, as well as the quartering of troops, constituted an *invasion* of the colonies. We can understand the situation better by a rough but still valid analogy. If today parliament were to assume the right to dissolve Canadian civil governments, to appoint officers, to legislate for Canada and to quarter troops there in case of resistance, it would constitute an invasion of a state which, beyond a common monarch and certain ties of empire and commonwealth, is a free and independent state. The thirteen colonies were free and independent states under their feudal lord, George III. They were not under parliament but had their own legislative bodies and their internally independent structures. The colonies had the right and power to issue their own money, a right which parliament sought to destroy. As early as 1606, in the First Charter of Virginia, it was declared:

> And that they shall, or lawfully may, establish and cause to be made a Coin, to pass current there between the peoples of those several Colonies, for the more Ease of Traffic and Bargaining between and amongst them and the Nations there, of such Metal, and in such Manner and Form, as the several Councils there shall limit and appoint.[10]

A state empowered to control and coin its own money is an independent state. The Crown did not reserve even to itself the right to coin money but saw that as a function of the local self-governments. The actions of parliament here and in other issues constituted an invasion of the colonies, and the actions of George III a violation of his feudal responsibilities. The Declaration of Independence accordingly never mentioned the British Parliament; they had no legal relationship thereto, and had no need to declare themselves independent of an authority they had never been subject to. There are two veiled references to this fact: "He (the king) has combined with others to subject us to a jurisdiction foreign to our constitution and unacknowledged by our laws, giving his assent to their pretended acts of legislation." The other reference to parliament is this: "We have warned them (our English brethren) . . . of attempts by their legislature to

---

[10] Richard L. Perry and John C. Cooper, editors: *Sources of Our Liberties*, p. 42. New York: American Bar Foundation, 1952.

extend an unwarrantable jurisdiction over us."[11]   The Declaration did cite the royal acts which rendered the king's feudal lordship over the colonies null and void.   Not the colonies but the king had rebelled against the prevailing law and order.   Legality was thus on the side of the colonists.   As the Declaration stated it, "The history of the present King of Great Britain is a history of repeated injuries and usurpations, all having in direct object the establishment of an absolute tyranny over these states."   And this was an accurate statement: parliamentary claims to absolute power were the issue, and royal assent thereto.   The legal meat of the Declaration is not in its opening generalities but in its specific demonstration that a legal, contractual and feudal relationship with George III had been violated and set aside by him, and the colonies invaded.   They were not in rebellion against the idea of a ruler, but against "a tyrant, . . . unfit to be the ruler of a free people."

Here again, having rebelled against centralism and absolutism, the states were not about to give to any federal government powers they would not tolerate in the hands of their mother country.   Indeed they had been more indulgent of the mother country than they were now ready to be of the federal government.   The purpose of the Constitution was thus not to create a strong central government, but, creating a federal union only sufficiently strong to maintain their unity, to thereupon limit it severely in order to prevent any future rise of centralism.   The Constitution accordingly makes 80 grants of power to the federal government while levying 115 prohibitions against it.   To the federal legislative authority, there are 20 grants of power and 70 restraints.   In addition, the express powers doctrine, implicit in the Constitution, is firmly spelled out in Amendments IX and X as a further check on the federal government.

In Amendment XI, the states asserted their further independence of federal jurisdiction.[12]

But it would be a serious error to assert that the alternative to federal sovereignty is State Rights.   Important as

---

[11] Carl L. Becker: *The Declaration of Independence*, A Study in the History of Political Ideas, pp. 18ff., 81ff., 104, 112, 131.   New York: Vintage Books, (1922), 1958.

[12] James Jackson Kilpatrick: *The Sovereign States*, pp. 53ff.   Chicago: Regnery, 1957.

the states are, they are not the basic unit of the American system. The basic unit is clearly and without question *the county;* significantly, one of the first steps towards independence was taken by Mecklenberg County, North Carolina, May 31, 1775, in order to prevent a legal vacuum.[13]

We have already noted that the county had certain powers with reference to religion. More important, in other areas the county had full jurisdiction, and these areas constitute the essence of civil government.

First, the *property tax* remained in the hands of the county, which had early established its jurisdiction. The people of an area thus controlled their tax assessor and their county supervisors, so that the taxing power was not beyond their jurisdiction. When the power to tax leaves the county, tyranny will then begin in the United States. Socialism or communism will be only a step away. The people of a county will be helpless as their property is taxed to the point of expropriation by a distant state capital. A step in this direction is already being contemplated in California. As yet, however, this all-important power remains for the most part with the county.

One of the central reasons for the Constitution was the failure of the Confederation because of its inability to tax, its Congress being dependent on the grants of the several states. While certain powers were removed from the United States of the Articles of Confederation by the Constitution, the central extension of power was the power to tax. This was circumscribed in two ways: first, debt paper money was barred, Congress and the states being limited to hard money and Congress being limited to coining money, regulating its value, and fixing the standard of weights and measures (Article I, Section 8). This power was moreover restricted to Congress, not to a central bank. Since debt paper money and inflation are forms of taxation, this was a severe limitation upon the powers of Congress, which had previously issued debt paper money, as had the states. Second, "no Capitation, or other direct tax" on the citizens, "unless in

---

[13] See Charles C. Tansill, ed.: *Documents Illustrative of the Formation of the Union of the American States,* pp. 6-9, 69th Congress, 1st Session, House Document no. 398. Washington: Government Printing Office, 1927. See also Perry and Cooper, *Sources of Our Liberties,* p. 314.

Proportion to the Census or Enumeration herein before directed to be taken," and "no tax or duty . . . on articles exported
from any state" (Article I Section 9), was permitted. Taxes
were essentially "Duties, Imposts and Excises" whose purpose
was "to pay the Debts and provide for the common Defense
and general Welfare of the United States" (Article I, Section
8). "General welfare" was clearly not intended to mean aid
to individuals and Madison so stated it in The Federalist.[14]
Thus, the most important area of taxation, property, was
left to the county, and income itself was regarded by the
Supreme Court as outside federal authority prior to the pas-
sage of the Sixteenth Amendment. In spite of the income
tax, the basic power still remains on the county level.

Second, *criminal law* was and is county law in essence.
This was an important safeguard against tyranny and against
the political use of criminal law. Law enforcement officers,
including judges, were and are officers of the county, in the
main, or of its constituent units. As T. Robert Ingram has
pointed out, not too many years ago executions were also
held at the county seat. Police power and criminal law are
thus matters of local jurisdiction in the American system.
This makes possible, on the moral decline of the community,
a slack enforcement of law and order, but, more than that,
it is the basic ingredient of liberty in the American legal
system, of self-government in both church and state. It is
local authority; it is self-government. It means truly that
which the jury system requires, trial by one's peers.

Third, *civil law* is also county law to a great degree,
enforced by local courts and by locally elected officials. The
American citizen is thus for the most part under county
government rather than state and federal government. His
basic instruments of civil government are local, residing in
the county, and the county is his historic line of defense
against the encroachments of state and federal governments.
In early America, town and county elections were properly
regarded as more important than state and federal elections,
and property qualifications more strict on the local level. The
county was the heart of the Protestant feudal restoration,

---

[14] Thomas James Norton: *The Constitution of the United States*,
p. 45. New York: America's Future, 1949. See James Madison: *The
Federalist* no. 41, p. 268f., Edward Mead Earle edition, New York:
Modern Library, 1936.

and the growth of state and especially federal power was as much distrusted as the growth of royal power and then royal absolutism had been hated and distrusted in an earlier era.

The county is currently under assault from United Nations, federal, state, and metropolitan planners.[15] City and county manager plans have been and are instrumental in subverting representative government and in undermining localism. Even as feudalism was and still is identified with backwardness and primitiveness, so the historic American system is now slandered as belonging to a horse and buggy age.

The first major assault on localism came very early, and it came from the states. The Constitution, in establishing the Electoral College, made it the exact numerical counterpart of Congress, with one elector for each congressional district and two at large for the two senators. The constitutional convention did not presume to order the states to follow the congressional districts strictly, with an elector named from each district, but it certainly suggested this by the exact coincidence of structure. It was assumed in the proceedings of the convention that prominent and able men from each congressional district, and from the state at large, would be elected or appointed as electors, and, to retain their independence and integrity, the electors could not be a "Senator or Representative, or person holding an office of trust or profit under the United States" (Article II, Section 1).

For some years, a variety of methods were used, and electors often had a measure of independence as well as ties to the local district. In 1836, however, the general ticket was used in every state except South Carolina (where election by the legislature continued until 1860), and rarely since then has there been a departure from the general ticket.[16]

State politicians had come to recognize the power inherent in the general ticket. Instead of binding each elector to the vote of the congressional district, with only the two at large bound to the state vote, the general ticket took the

---

[15] See E. G. Grace: *What Is Metropolitan Government?*, Los Angeles, 1958; Jo Hindman: *Terrible 1313 Revisited*, Caldwell, Idaho: Caxton Press, 1963. See also *Don Bell Reports*, Year Ten, nos. 7-10, Feb. 15, 22, March 1, 1963.

[16] Karl E. Mundt, "Is Your Presidential Vote Worth MORE or LESS than your Neighbor's?" in *Dawn*, September, 1962, VII, 7, pp. 4, 6. Portland, Indiana.

power from the congressional district, the local unit, and gave it to the state. As a result, while every congressional district in a state except those of the large urban center may vote for one candidate, their votes are nullified by the slim majority given by the urban vote, and *all* electoral votes can go to the other candidate.

The state politicians were not alone in recognizing the power inherent in the general ticket. *Minority groups* quickly recognized that it gave them *the balance of power* between the two parties. The first group to make use of this power was the Abolitionist movement. Slavery had previously been a source of tension but had been very far from dominating federal politics. Now the picture changed rapidly. A few thousand abolitionists, for example, in New York State could, by throwing their vote to one party or another, decide the outcome of an election.

In New York State, the legislature for over thirty years after 1792 chose the electors, the excuse for the legal provision thereof in 1792 being that "there was not sufficient time prior to the election of 1792 to make arrangements for a popular choice of electors." In 1824, when the demand for popular election mounted, there were 260,000 voters and 160 state legislators in New York. Governor Yates expected an amendment to the U.S. Constitution to correct the situation and require district election. After much struggle, popular pressure led to a change to the election of electors by districts as against (1) election by legislature, (2) election on a general ticket with a plurality vote, or (3) election on a general ticket with a majority vote. New York went on the general ticket system in the election of 1832.[17] On the general ticket plan, only a few thousand votes were needed to swing the state for a particular candidate; hence the bargaining power of the minority groups.

The New York vote, 1824 to 1836, is instructive in this regard. In the 1824 presidential election, the New York electoral vote was as follows, with the legislature choosing the electors: Jackson 1, Adams 26, Crawford 5, Clay 4. In 1828, with districts electing the electors, the results were as follows: Jackson, 140,763 votes, 50.97% of the vote, 20 elec-

---

[17] C. H. Rammelkamp, "The Campaign of 1824 in New York," *Annual Report of the American Historical Association for the Year 1904*, pp. 175-201. Washington: Government Printing Office, 1905.

tors; Adams, 135,413 votes, 49.03% of the vote, 16 electors. In 1832, with the general ticket system, Jackson received 168,562 votes or 52.11%, and 42 electoral votes, while Clay, who received 154,986 votes, or 47.89%, received no electoral votes. In 1836, Van Buren took all 42 electoral votes also on 166,886 votes, 54.60%, while Harrison with 138,765 votes, or 45.40%, received no electoral votes.[18] The significance of this fact, that a bloc vote of a few thousand could dictate to either party or any candidate certain terms in return for their vote, was not lost on politicians or on minority groups. Control had passed out of the hands of the reasonable majorities on either side into the hands of the unbending single-issue minorities. In many areas, these groups early took control.

The effect on national politics was devastating. The slavery issue was forced upon both parties, and upon Congress, by the ability of the minority to control the outcome in state elections. The effect upon the parties was also shattering. The National Democracy increasingly became a Southern party. The Whigs were broken because of their temporizing on the issue, and the Republican Party was born, a party which in 1860 elected a minority president, Lincoln, and which was itself dominated, not by its majority but by a minority. The Civil War was thus a product of the rise to power of a minority through the general ticket.

Since then, the minority power has been consistently used as the chief instrument of power. Various groups were effective from the Civil War to Franklin Delano Roosevelt, but, since Roosevelt, this instrument has been especially refined. Minority groups, by means of the general ticket, hold the balance of power in many states: the labor vote, Negroes, Catholics, Zionist Jews, pensioners, and the like. Candidates campaign accordingly, not for the vote of the majority of Republicans and Democrats, but for the "swing vote," the minority and single-issue voter who now governs American politics. Only by restoring localism, by amending the Constitution to require the coincidence of the electoral college and its vote with the structure of Congress, can minority rule, with its attendant evils, hatred and injustice, be checked.

---

[18] Svend Petersen: *A Statistical History of the American Presidential Elections*, pp. 18-23. New York: Frederick Ungar, 1963.

We have seen the two causes of the Revolution, the religious issue and the invasion of localism and self-government, and the implications of these positions for us today.

Let us now examine some other aspects of American history which clearly distinguished the American system then from what it is today. Important among these was the attitude towards *property and suffrage*. The question of a federal requirement of property for suffrage was earnestly raised at the Convention by several men. Gouverneur Morris objected to the rule of numbers alone as against property, stating, "not liberty, property is the main object of society." Rutledge agreed: "Property is certainly the principal object of society." King said, "Property is the primary object of society, and in fixing a ratio, ought not to be excluded from the estimate." Butler held that "Property is the only just measure of representation." James Wilson clearly disagreed: "Property is not the sole nor the primary end of government and society; the improvement of the human mind is the most noble object." Madison held that such a federal measure would establish class hostility in the United States while evading the fact that "landed possessions were no certain evidence of real wealth," many landowners being deeply in debt. Benjamin Franklin pointed out several objections to the property qualification, warning, "Remember, the scripture requires in rulers that they should be men hating covetousness."[19] Dickinson opposed the qualification, since a constitutional statement would not be complete and yet would limit Congress "from supplying the omissions." Moreover, "The best defense lay in the freeholders who were to elect the Legislature. Whilst this Source should remain pure, the public interest would be safe. If it ever should be corrupt, no little expedients would repel the danger."[20] A federal requirement of property was thus defeated, and the matter left in the hands of the states and counties.

Madison was not certain exactly what the answer to the problem of qualified suffrage was, but he felt "the freeholders

---

[19] George Bancroft: *History of the Formation of the Constitution of the United States of America*, vol II pp. 69f., 85, 91f., 125-128. New York: Appleton, 1882.

[20] Charles C. Tansill, ed.: *Documents Illustrative of the Formation of the Union of the American States*, p. 460 (Debates as reported by James Madison).

of the Country would be the safest depositories of Republican liberty." He foresaw the time when, unlike the situation in his day, many voters would be property-less workingmen who would become "the tools of opulence and ambition." The result would be a European style aristocracy.[21] Gouveneur Morris feared the same thing: "unless you establish a qualification of Property, we shall have an aristocracy."[22] The demand for a property qualification was thus as a preventative to aristocracy or oligarchy, the plunder of the people by the rich few in the name of the masses. Much later, a master politician stated what was necessary for the triumph of an oligarchy. Franklin Delano Roosevelt declared:

> Now, to bring about government by oligarchy masquerading as democracy, it is fundamentally essential that practically all authority and control be centralized in our National Government.[23]

Property qualifications, of varying degrees, existed on the state level. They tended to be even more strict on the local and county level, where the property tax was involved. To give voting rights over property to non-propertied men was seen as destructive of law and order. Since, Cooper stated, "The governments of towns and villages, for instance, are almost entirely directed to the regulation of property, and to the control of local interests," suffrage should be restricted to the propertied, who have a stake in the issues involved.[24] In some areas today, separate ballots exist for property owners, who alone can vote on bond issues and like measures. The mainspring of many conservative movements of the 1950's and 1960's is the revolt of property owners against equalitarian and confiscatory measures.

The issue with respect to property was perhaps most sharply stated in 1843 by Karl Marx. It should be noted that his references to "the state" mean thereby, except in reference to American states, the modern *secular* state.

---

[21] *Ibid.*, p. 489f.

[22] *Ibid.*, p. 874.

[23] *The Public Papers and Addresses of Franklin D. Roosevelt*, vol. I, *The Genesis of the New Deal*, 1928-1932, "Radio Address on States' Rights," March 2, 1930, pp. 569-575; New York: Random House, 1938. See also *N.Y. Times*, p. 1, March 3, 1930, "Roosevelt Decries Waning State Rule."

[24] James Fenimore Cooper: *The American Democrat*, p. 136. (1838) New York: Vintage Books, 1956.

The state is the intermediary between man and his free-dom. As Christ is the intermediary whom the Christian burdens with his divinity and all his religious ties, so the state is the intermediary whom man burdens with his entire non-divinity and his complete absence of ties.

The political triumph of man over religion shares all the advantages and disadvantages of political triumph generally. Thus, for example, the state annuls private property: man proclaims politically that private proper-ty is abolished as soon as he abolishes the property quali-fication for the vote, as has been done in several Ameri-can states. . . . Is not private property as an idea abolished when the non-owner becomes legislator for the owner? The property qualification for the vote is the ultimate political form of the recognition of private property.[25]

Some points of very great importance are here asserted or implied. First, as the state grows in its power, it "emancipates itself from religion" and professes "no religion except its own statehood."[26] This secular state accordingly becomes man's "intermediary" or mediator and man's savior. The state be-comes the road to paradise regained and the source of man's salvation. The secular state is thus inevitably a messianic order. Second, "the state annuls private property." "The state can be a free state without the man in it being a free man."[27] It is certainly significant that in the United States today there is increasing reference to our status as "a free nation" and less to our heritage as a free people, free individuals. For the state to be *free,* requires us to ask, free from whom? The state wants to be free, not only from foreign powers, but, most commonly of all, from bondage to its own people. *To free itself, the state must enslave its citizens.* To do this, it must, first, secularize itself and the people, and, second, annul private property, since both Chris-tianity and property give the citizenry an independence of the state and keep the state strictly limited.

Third, Marx pointed out, "private property as an idea" is "abolished when the non-owner becomes legislator for the owner." How long would Christianity last as an institution if unbelievers could vote in churches? Will non-owners re-

---

[25] Karl Marx: *A World Without Jews,* p. 10f. Trans, with intro. and epilogue by Dagobert D. Runes. Fourth, enlarged edition. New York: Philosophical Library, 1960.

[26] *Ibid.,* p. 9.

[27] *Ibid.,* p. 10.

spect property to any greater degree? The answer is the steady confiscation of wealth, property and income through taxation. As of June, 1963, federal, state, and local civilian workers exceeded 12 million, with another 28 million receiving welfare in one form or another. Federal executive civilian employees numbered 2,353,054; legislative, 22,853; judicial, 4,900; for a total of 2,380,807. The total revenue of federal, state, and local civil governments exceeded $150 billions a year. Since one in seven persons is a welfare beneficiary, the burden of this taxation falls heavily on the responsible citizenry. The rise of statism coincides with the decline of faith, of private property, and of responsibility. And to speed its rise to power, the state must further erode these things and is hence by nature hostile to them.

In no other area has so radical a change taken place from the early years of the United States as in *education*. The "public school" movement, or statist education, did not exist until the 1830's. Statist education began as a subversive movement and its bitter, savage struggle has not yet been written.[28] The essentials of the drive which produced statist education are clearly seen in Horace Mann (1796-1859), "the Father of the Common Schools." First and foremost, Mann was a Unitarian. New England Unitarianism was in the forefront of the battle for statist education. For Mann, Unitarianism was true Christianity, and, with humorless zeal, he fought for his holy faith. The direction of Unitarian thought had been very early charted by William Ellery Channing. According to Phillips, for Channing, "the secular organization of society usually takes the place of Divine Society on earth, historically the Christian Church, and itself becomes the agent of God's salvation." Channing moved towards "the divinization of the national state," stating in 1812 "that government is a divine institution." The biblical position is that civil government is divinely ordained or instituted but definitely not itself divine; indeed, biblical faith is at war with such a position. But Channing, by 1830, held to "a completely univocal community, with all human and divine sanc-

---

[28] This writer has written of the history of the philosophies of education in that struggle. See R. J. Rushdoony: *The Messianic Character of American Education;* Nutley, N. J.: Craig Press, 1963.

tions."[29]   For Channing, according to Phillips, "Man's salvation, then, is to be worked out not on the basis of membership in the mystical body of Christ, but citizenship in the glorious race of mankind."[30]   For Theodore Parker, another Unitarian leader, the true church was the great invisible Church of Mankind, to be revealed through America. O. B. Frothingham subsequently (1872) affirmed "The Religion of Humanity" and his hopes in "the new paradise" to be brought in by the state.   In view of this very extensive Unitarian movement, it is not surprising that its members and friends saw the old Christian school as backward and incapable of dealing with the basic issues of the times.   True education had to be concerned with *liberty,* and the order of man's liberty was the *state.* This Horace Mann affirmed fervently. The responsibility of the church was libertarian rather than salvationist, and freedom was institutional, i.e., statist in nature. As a result, education was properly the province of the state. Mann labored, therefore, to free the schools from their basically Christian and independent nature in order to give them true direction, as he saw it, in terms of the state. His hostility against the Calvinism and against the free schools of the day was thus bitter and intense. Education, to fulfill its calling, *had* to be statist. State schools would, he believed, render most sin, crime, poverty, ignorance, and prisons obsolete in a century.

Second, Horace Mann, was not, in the modern sense, a socialist but he did hold to the premises of that position. According to Merle Curti, Mann had naive misconceptions about socialism.[31]   While it would be an error to apply the full modern sense of the word socialist to Mann, it is clear that his answers to social problems were basically statist. While, in terms of current practice, Mann was in many things "conservative," he was, by his acceptance of the state as the univocal order of man, radically committed to a socialized order, of which the school was the first and the basic part. Moreover, the conversion of America's education into an instru-

---

[29] Clifton J. Phillips: *Puritan and Unitarian Views of Church and Society in America,* p. I 4f. Unpublished thesis, Starr King School for the Ministry (Unitarian), Berkeley, California, June, 1944.

[30] Phillips, p. I 6.

[31] Merle Curti: *The Social Ideas of American Educators,* p. 120. Paterson, New Jersey: Littlefield, Adams, 1959.

ment of statism was the most important step into socialism which a society can ever take, for to socialize the child is a far more radical step than to socialize income, monetary wealth, or property. It was therefore precisely what the Beards termed it, "the educational revolution," that Mann effected.[32]

Unitarianism on the whole prided itself on its socialism. Prominent Unitarians were instrumental in the many social-istic enthusiasms of the 1840's, and Brook Farm, according to Noyes, "in its original conception, was not a Fourier forma-tion at all, but an American seedling. It was the child of New England Unitarianism."[33] State controlled education was one of a number of causes Unitarianism championed; temperance, peace, and abolition, among other causes, also inflamed these humorless reformers. Their answer to all these problems, and many more, was statist action. Behind John Brown, who was subsidized to start warfare, stood his sponsors, the Secret Six, Unitarians.[34] John Brown's hanging was compared to Jesus's crucifixion by Thoreau, and Edouard de Stoeckl, the Russian Minister, wrote to his government that Brown was being "proclaimed . . . as the equal of our Savior."[35]

[32] Charles A. and Mary R. Beard: *The Rise of American Civiliza-tion*, I, p. 816. New York: Macmillan, 1930. Sumner, enthusiastically supporting Mann, declared, "Let us put an iron heel upon the serpent of religious bigotry trying to hug our schools in its insidious coil," David Donald: *Charles Sumner and the Coming of the Civil War*, p. 87; New York: Knopf, 1961.

[33] John Humphrey Noyes: *History of American Socialisms*, p. 104. (1870) New York: Hilary House, 1961.

[34] J. C. Furnas: *The Road to Harpers Ferry*. New York: William Sloane, 1959. Thomas Wentworth Higginson (1823-1911), a Unitarian clergyman and one of the Secret Six, remarked in early 1858 to one of "Old Brown's" appeals for money: "I am always ready to invest money in treason, but at present have none to invest," Furnas, p. 337. Early in his long and dedicated career, Higginson had been a zealous supporter of Horace Mann, Furnas, p. 338. He lived long enough to sponsor many a radical movement, and was, in 1905, with Clarence S. Darrow, Jack London, Upton Sinclair and six others, the signers of the September 12 "Call" which started the Intercollegiate Socialist Society. On Higgin-son, as on other Unitarians of his era, the influences of French Revolu-tionary thought and English Fabianism were extensive. For the "Call" see Mina Weisenberg: *The L.I.D., Fifty Years of Democratic Educa-tion*, 1905-1955, New York: League for Industrial Democracy, 1955.

[35] Edmund Wilson: *Patriotic Gore*, Studies in the Literature of the American Civil War, p. 246. New York: Oxford, 1962.

This was the Unitarian ethos in which Horace Mann moved. Some Unitarians gave themselves over to fighting for peace, others for abolition, feminism, and the like. Mann's statist panacea was government control of schools. It should be added that, as a dedicated advocate of phrenology, he was already committed to the faith that a man's life was essentially governed by external factors, a first principle of statist salvation.

The concept of "democratic" or statist education has waged war, not only against the Christian faith, but against the family as well. Very early, by the 1860's California made criticism of a teacher by a "parent, guardian, or other person . . . in the presence or hearing of a pupil thereof, . . . a misdemeanor." Other states had also elevated the authority of the teacher above that of parents.[36]   After World War II, James Bryant Conant wrote:

> Wherever the institution of the family is still a powerful force, as it is in this country, surely *inequality* of opportunity is automatically, and often unconsciously, a basic principal of the nation; the more favored parents endeavor to obtain even greater favors for their children. Therefore, when we Americans proclaim an adherence to the doctrine of equality of opportunity we face the necessity for a perpetual compromise. Now it seems to me important to recognize both the inevitable conflict and the continuing nature of the compromise.[37]

The "public" or statist schools, which began their history as a subversive movement, aimed at subverting the old order, now cast the implication of subversion on the family! It should be remembered that the family was once the primary educational institution. As late as 1883, a parental guide book, faced with the spread of state schools, urged, "Parents will do wisely, wherever it is possible, to carry on the work of elementary instruction at home."[38]   In the 1950's, when highly qualified parents did this and did it ably, they were haled into courts. Statist education is intolerant increasingly of any rivalry.

---

[36] Zach. Montgomery: *The School Question from a Parental and Non-Secretarian Stand-Point*, p. 51.   Washington: Gibson, 1886.

[37] James Bryant Conant: *Education in a Divided World*, The Function of the Public Schools in our Unique Society, p. 8.   Cambridge: Harvard University Press. 1948.

[38] John Hall: *A Christian Home: How to Make and How to Maintain It*, p. 77 Philadelphia: American Sunday School Union 1883.

But, in recent years, a steady revolt against statist education has been developing, with as many as 16% of all grade and high school students enrolled in non-state schools by 1960. This has been the one area where the advance of statism has been turned into a retreat. The threat, however, of a major offensive is very real. State, federal, and United Nation agencies seek control over *every* kind of school, statist and non-statist, in the name of "humanity." The necessary implication is too seldom faced by Americans: the need to attack by advocating the outright abolition of all statist schools as inimical to liberty. Unfortunately, the only county so to move, Prince Edward County, Virginia, did so in 1958 for a reason other than the issue of statism, i.e., the U. S. Fourth Circuit of Appeals order for desegregation of the county's high schools.[39] There is reason to believe, however, that the heyday of the "public" school is ended, and that free schools will eventually supplant it, although not without struggle. But it needs to be remembered that statist and secular education was not a part of the American system for the first two centuries of its history, including its first forty years under the Constitution, and, even then, was viewed for some time as a radical and dangerous innovation.

Another vastly different aspect of the current scene, reflecting the change in the American system, concerns welfare. An adequate history of welfare does not exist. The major role of the medieval church, and especially of various orders, in ministering to the sick and needy, is too little known. Extensive foundations and trust funds for these purposes were confiscated by the national states, and the "modern" era began with major problems of charity as a result. Gradually, churches, private associations, trusts and foundations assumed the responsibility and met it. The activity of the civil government in this area was almost entirely limited to the county, and was limited in its jurisdiction.[40]

---

[39] *Ebony*, vol. XIX, no. 1, November, 1963, pp. 63-66, 68.

[40] For an interesting account of one such measure, the poor vendu, see Samuel Hopkins Adams: *Grandfather Stories*, pp. 231ff.; New York: Signet, 1955. See also *The Life-Line . . or Autobiography of Warren Chase*, pp. 19, 22-32. For an important study of an aspect of the English history of Welfare, see W. K. Jordan: *Philanthropy in England, 1480-1660*, A Study of Changing Pattern of English Social Aspirations, London: George Allen and Unwin, 1959.

The transition from the older to the current situation can best be analyzed by briefly examining Kansas City in 1909. In autumn, when thousands were unemployed, the Helping Hand Institute set up rock quarrying and breaking operations, with the rock sold to the city for road work. The help thus provided was insufficient to meet the emergency. Wealthy citizens, led by William Volker, worked to create the first municipal Department of Public Welfare, April 4, 1910. This public agency, however, was still supported by private funds, Volker funds, so that it was still, as in the past, a case of organized private charity meeting all needs and problems. This Department set up a loan agency for the needy, confronted the problems of prostitution and immorality, and sought to co-ordinate the work of private agencies, such as the Helping Hand Institute and the Provident Association, and to meet needs not covered by existing private agencies. After Volker left the Department in April, 1911, it became in fact a *municipal* agency, and politicians like Thomas J. Pendergast recognized its potentiality as *an instrument of political power.* Volker himself "learned that government and politics are inseparable, by definition; that political charity is not charity at all." He observed in 1918, when the last member of the independent board, Leroy Halbert, was ousted by "the machine-dominated City Council," "I've learned something about government. . . Government must be restricted to those activities which can be entrusted to the worst citizens, not the best."[41]

Other cities very rapidly followed Kansas City in establishing departments of public welfare; states, and then the federal government, quickly followed suit. The tremendous potentialities for political power were widely recognized. *Not charity but power* is the primary function of statist welfare. The attempts of various agencies in recent years to move faster than the public demand, and then to create by propaganda that public demand, is motivated by a lust for power, not by a regard for human welfare. Charity is a by-product: there must be enough, like bread and circuses, to keep the masses happy, but the foremost goal is power, power to be gods and to manipulate men and society, to indulge the whims of megalomania in the name of benevolence.

---

[41] Herbert C. Cornuelle: *"Mr. Anonymous,"* The Story of William Volker, p. 78. Chicago: Regnery, 1951.

And with this goes a re-writing of history. It is not surprising that some college students are beginning to report, unfortunately with credulity, that they are taught that, after the 1929 economic depression, hungry mobs went rampaging in the streets, and people dropped to the sidewalks of America in the last stages of hunger.

It is clear-cut that a second American Revolution has taken place. In the words of Garet Garrett's title, *The Revolution Was,* and it is now trying to extirpate the citizen's memory of the first revolution. This second revolution is a kind of return to Europe, to "the house of bondage," a rebellion against liberty and its responsibilities. It is not surprising that it has gone hand in hand with either a debunking of or ignorance concerning the American Revolution and its background. For the restoration of that first revolution, *and its extension,* there must first be a return to a Christian faith, a faith that not the state but Christ is the Savior and Mediator, and, second, a return to the Protestant restoration of feudalism, to the centrality and importance of the local unit, the county and its elements.

CHAPTER II

FISHER AMES: THE RESPONSIBILITY
OF THE MINORITY

One of the neglected men of American history is Fisher Ames (1758-1808). Apart from his dates, one biographical dictionary has only this to report concerning him: American politician, born at Dedham, Mass., member of congress, orator."[1] He is also remembered at times as the man who declined the presidency of Harvard.

Fisher Ames was in his day the great and eloquent voice of Federalism, with John Adams its vocal philosopher. Because of his power in congress, he was the object of the first purge attempted in the history of the United States under the Constitution. Thomas Jefferson had singled Ames out for defeat, hoping that this "colossus of the monocrats and paper men" would be retired from the House. But Ames, on November 2, 1792, was re-elected to the Third Congress by an overwhelming vote, receiving 1,627 out of the 2,900 votes cast, and receiving "almost twice as many votes as Benjamin Austin Jr., once more his chief opponent."[2]

What Jefferson could not do, history, by its changing perspective, has done, namely, purged Fisher Ames from his place of eminence. One is almost grateful to Parrington for having, in spite of his supercilious treatment, at least given renewed attention to Ames.[3]

Ames, who held the galleries spellbound with his relentless logic and great eloquence, is able to command his readers

---

[1] *Chambers' Biographical Dictionary*, J. O. Thorne, ed., p. 33. New York: St. Martin's Press, 1962.

[2] Barnes Riznik: *The Eloquent Fisher Ames: Zealot of the Massachusetts Federalists*, p. 113f. Unpublished thesis, Stanford University, April, 1960.

[3] Vernon Louis Parrington: *Main Currents in American Thought*, vol. II, pp. 279-288. New York: Harcourt, Brace, 1930.

today. It is readily understandable to readers why only his poor health and enforced retirement prevented him from exercising an even more important role in American history.

According to his son Seth, "Mr. Ames apprehended that our government has been sliding down from a true republic toward the abyss of democracy: and that the ambition of demagogues operating on personal, party, and local passions, was attaining its objects."[4] Fisher Ames did not place his trust in abstractions or in documents; constitutionalist though he was, he could declare, "Constitutions are but paper; society is the substratum of government." The "best security" was the old, conservative New England society he knew.[5] In 1801 he limited it more sharply: "Connecticut is the life-guard of liberty and federalism."[6] Ames, it should be noted, was a Massachusetts man.

Ames was deeply concerned over the organized subversion coming into America from the French Revolution, and the readiness of some to accept these opinions. Whatever the French did against Christianity, the United States, and humanity, "we stand ready to approve all they do, and to approve more than they can do. This French mania is the bane of our politics, the mortal poison that makes our peace so sickly. It is incurable by any other remedy than time."[7] By 1799, time had aided the situation, as the French picture became more obviously one of savage disorder, and Ames could observe: "Public opinion is the real sovereign of our country, and not a very capricious one neither. France is neither loved nor trusted. . . We begin to feel a little patriotism. . . ."[8] The causes of Europe's sickness were, as Ames saw it, very deep, and likely to corrupt America also, whose chance of escaping the infection rested in part on Europe's ability to overcome its sickness. "The morbid cause of the

---

[4] *Works of Fisher Ames, with a Selection from His Speeches and Correspondence*, edited by his son Seth Ames, Vol. I, p. 22. Boston: Little, Brown, 1854.

[5] *Idem.*

[6] Ames, I, p. 295, letters to Theodore Dwight, Dedham, March 19, 1801.

[7] Ames, I, p. 139f. Letters to Christopher Gore, Philadelphia, March 26, 1794.

[8] Ames, I, p. 254, Letter to Timothy Pickering, Dedham, March 12, 1799.

French Revolution lies deep; it is not a rash on the skin; it is a plague that makes the bones brittle and cankers the marrow. The disease is not medicable." War was needed to educate men "in the ancient manly virtues," and a new generation with a different perspective. "As to liberty we are to have none—democracy will kindle its own hell, and consume in it."[9] By 1807, he was again fearful of the triumph of the French power, and of Jacobinism in America.

Ames was a man of his time and echoed many of its pat phrases: he was ready on one occasion to see as "a fixed rule and standard of political conduct . . . the greatest permanent happiness of the greatest number of people."[10] On the other hand, he was ready to contrast the rule of law with the rule of the popular will: "The Washington and Adams administration proceeded on the basis that the government was organized, and clothed with power to rule according to the Constitution; the democratic theorists insist, that the people, meaning themselves, have a good right to rule."[11] Ames, coming from democratic Massachusetts' small town society, was a bitter foe of democracy and spoke bluntly of its defects:

> All democrats maintain that the people have an inherent, unalienable right to power; there is nothing so fixed that they may not change it; nothing so sacred that their voice, which is the voice of God, would not unsanctify and consign to destruction; it is not only true that no king, or parliament, or generation past, can bind the people, but they cannot even bind themselves; the will of the majority is not only law, but right; having an unlimited right to act as they please, whatever they please to act is a rule. Thus virtue itself, thus public faith, thus common honesty, are no more than arbitrary rules which the people have, as yet, abstained from rescinding; and when a confiscating or paper-money majority in congress should ordain otherwise, they would be no longer rules. Hence the worshippers of this idol ascribe to it attributes inconsistent with all our ideas of the Supreme Being himself, to whom we deem it equally impious and absurd to impute injustice. Hence they argue that a public debt is a burden to be thrown off whenever the people grow weary of it; and hence they

---

[9] Ames, I, p. 367, Letter to Timothy Pickering, Dedham, March 3, 1806.

[10] Ames, II, p. 108, "Political Essays," Camillus No. III.

[11] Ames, II, p. 140, Falkland No. III, "To New England Men."

somewhat inconsistently pretend that the very people cannot make a constitution authorizing any restraint upon malicious lying against the government. So that, according to them, neither religion, nor morals, nor policy, nor the people themselves can erect any barrier against the reasonable or the capricious exercise of their power. Yet, what these cannot do, the spirit of sedition can; this is more sacred than religion, or justice, and dearer than the general good itself. For it is evident, that if we will have the unrestricted liberty of lying against our magistrates, and laws, and government, we can have no other liberty; and the clamorous Jacobins have decided that such liberty, without any other, is better than every other kind of liberty without it.

Is it true, however, (if it be not rebellion to inquire) that this uncontrolled power of the people is their right, and that it is absolutely essential to their liberty? All our individual rights are to be exercised with due regard to the rights of others; they are tied fast by restrictions, and are to be exercised within certain reasonable limits. How is it, then, that the democrats find a right in the whole people so much more extensive than what belongs to any one of their number? In other cases, the extremes of any principle are so many departures from principle. Why is it, then, that they make popular right to consist wholly in extremes, and that so absolutely, that without such boundless pretensions they say it could not subsist at all? Checks on the people themselves are not merely clogs, but chains. They are usurpations which should be abolished, even if in practice they prove useful; for, they will tell you, precedent sanctions and introduces tyranny. Neither Commodus nor Caligula were ever so flattered with regard to the extent of their power, and the impiety of setting bounds to it, as any people who listen to demagogues.

The writings of Thomas Paine and the democratic newspapers will evince that this representation of their doctrine is not caricatured; it is not more extravagant than they represent it themselves. They often, indeed, affirm that they are not admirers of a mere democracy; they know it will prove licentious; they are in favor of an energetic government.[12]

Ames held that a study of the French Revolution was necessary as an example of the logical course of democracy, and of revolution as well. He recognized how *essential* revolution was to this faith as a cure-all for all past ills: "Every

[12] Ames, II, Equality no. III, p. 213f.

democrat more or less firmly believes that a revolution is
the sure path to liberty; and therefore he believes government
of little importance to the people, and a very great impediment to their rights."[13] Tyranny gains its foothold by appeal-
ing to the evil in man; the tyrant cannot function alone;
he must interest "a sufficient number of subordinate tyrants
in the duration of his power."[14] The people are enlisted by
assaulting property, "the object of the great mass of every
faction." Gradually, not only the propertied but the masses
will be stripped of every private right and privilege. When
this happens, "there is no return to liberty. What the fire
of faction does not destroy, it will debase." Slaves of this
sort may dislike their slavery, but it is the outcome of their
own lusts and demands.[15] Eventually, testing would come
to the American people, as it must come to all. It cannot
be otherwise. But "we seem to expect a state of felicity
before a state of probation. Of our six millions of people
there are scarcely six hundred who yet look for liberty anywhere except on paper."[16]

The Federalists had been seriously in error. They assumed as a *natural* fact a *moral* product, character. "Federalism was therefore manifestly founded on a mistake, on the
supposed existence of sufficient political virtue, and on the
permanency and authority of the public morals. The party
now in power committed no such mistake. They acted on
the knowledge of what men actually are, not what they ought
to be. Instead of enlightening the popular understanding,
their business was to bewilder it."[17] But, "a democracy cannot last." It will then change "into a military despotism";
an imperialism will be the outcome. Moreover, as democracy
moves into empire, empire does not stand still. "Experience
proves, that in all such governments there is a continual
tendency to unity."[18] "Ought we not then to be convinced,
that something more is necessary to preserve liberty than to

[13] Ames, II, p. 223, Equality No. VI, "The Nature and Basis of
Bonaparte's Power."
[14] Ames, II, p. 280f., "The Combined Powers and France."
[15] Ames, II, p. 368f., "The Dangers of American Liberty."
[16] Ames, I, Letter to Timothy Pickering, Dedham, November 6, 1807,
p. 397f.
[17] Ames, II, p. 379, "The Dangers of American Liberty."
[18] *Ibid.*, p. 382.

love it? Ought we not to see that when the people have destroyed all power but their own, they are the nearest possible to a despotism, the more uncontrolled for being new, and tenfold the more cruel for its hypocrisy?"[19]

Ames was, as Parrington charged, a champion of property, but by this Ames did not mean moneyed wealth, but a land-based people, whose property, business and agricultural, was not a paper-based, credit-based wealth, but established on character and production. His picture of the future was not a hopeful one.

> But the condition of the United States is changing. Luxury is sure to introduce want; and the great inequalities between the very rich and the very poor will be more conspicuous, and comprehend a more formidable host of the latter. The rabble of great cities is the standing army of ambition. Money will become its instrument, and vice its agent. Every step, (and we have taken many) towards a more complete, unmixed democracy is an advance toward destruction; it is treading where the ground is treacherous and excavated for an explosion. Liberty has never yet lasted long in a democracy; nor has it ever ended in any thing better than despotism. With the change of our government, our manners and sentiments will change. As soon as our emperor has destroyed his rivals, and established order in his army, he will desire to see splendor in his court, and to occupy his subjects with the cultivation of the sciences.[20]

The power of evil is always the greater where men lack the faith and character which makes them move in terms of truth rather than a lie. "Suppose a missionary should go to the Indians and recommend self-denial and the ten commandments, and another should exhort them to drink rum, who would first convert the heathen? Yet we are told, the vox populi is the vox dei; and our demagogues claim a right divine to reign over us."[21]

Very early, Ames knew the reality of the American scene, that good, strong character was lacking in most. When Indians attacked settlers in one area, Congress began to move for their relief through the army. But these "back settlers"

---

[19] *Ibid.*, p. 395.

[20] Ames, II, p. 441f., "American Literature."

[21] Ames, I, p. 316f. Letter to Jeremiah Smith, Boston, December 14, 1802.

had a better idea than their relief and rescue: an opportunity to tap the public treasury in return for defending their own homes and families! "They wish to be hired as volunteers, at two thirds of a dollar a day, to fight the Indians. They would drain the Treasury."[22]

What was Ames' answer? It was twofold. First, there was needed "the miracle of virtue, that loves others first, then one's self."[23] Here Ames revealed the transition of the New England faith from piety to moralism. He was himself a part of the theological decline in that he saw Christianity in terms of the Edwardian general benevolence rather than justifying faith.

Second, Ames felt that even a small minority can exercise great power if it moves in terms of principle. In 1807, with the Federalist eclipse, he could assert, "Even now, federalism checks, though it cannot govern. It is fitter to check than to rule. . . . . It is better to suffer the fatigue of pumping, than to sit sullen till the ship sinks."[24]

More can be said on this matter. History has never been commanded by majorities but always by dedicated minorities. We have seen the havoc wrought in American history by minority groups playing their balance of power game. This was not what Ames had in mind. Rather, he held to the responsibility of the privileged minority, and for him the privileged minority was made up of people like those whom he knew and loved best, his New England neighbors, men of simple faith and strong virtues.

The Revolution, we have been told, was fought as a "minority war," with perhaps one-third more or less loyal to George III, one third indifferent, and the other third in favor of resistance to the invading troops. This estimate may or may not be accurate, but what is true is that at first only a dedicated minority recognized the implications of their defense of liberty and was ready to face those implications. There were gradually men ready to pledge their lives, their fortunes, and their sacred honor to the cause, but, before the people followed, there first came the dedicated minority.

---

[22] Ames, I, p. 109, Letter to Thomas Dwight, Philadelphia, January 13, 1792.

[23] Ames, I, p. 377f. Letter to Richard Peters, December 14, 1806.

[24] Ames, I, p. 401, Letter to Josiah Quincy, Dedham, November 19, 1807.

We can, thus, with slight alteration, agree with Ames' analysis and answer. First is needed the miracle of *faith*, and then the dedicated minority. Already, that minority checks, although it cannot govern.

CHAPTER III

ALEXANDER H. STEPHENS: CONSTITUTIONALISM VERSUS CENTRALISM

In his day, Fisher Ames had many of the defects of the Federalism of New England; Alexander Hamilton Stephens (1812-1883) was associated with many causes which serve to disqualify him of interest and appeal to most people today. The desire is for heroes or thinkers who make no mistakes and lose no battles; as a result, men get figureheads and compromisers. It is thus no wonder then that so important an American political thinker as Stephens has suffered from neglect. He was a Southerner who defended slavery, a fact which makes present-day conservatives shy away from him. On the other hand, Stephens opposed secession, and, although vice-president of the Confederacy, has been called near treasonable in his hostility to that civil government. In many respects, he was closer in temperament to intellectuals than to politicians, but his every opinion puts a gap between him and the modern intellectuals. On these and many other counts, Stephens stands as an isolated figure.

But, for many reasons, Stephens is important to the United States. For one thing, his life serves to illustrate why the war was a *Civil* War. Southerners are clearly technically correct in calling it the *War Between the States*. Politically, it was precisely that, and it would seem clear that Stephens had the better of the argument in so terming it. Until that war ended, the United States was to a very great extent accepted on all sides as a confederation of states, and many Northern leaders were of the opinion that the South was free to go. Lincoln warned of a "civil war" in his First Inaugural Address, but the juridicial precedents favored a federal rather than a national construction of the civil order.

Stephens was thus right politically, but only politically.   In a tragic sense, it was *civil* war.   In very many ways, North and South then were characterized by a greater racial and cultural unity than the United States has since possessed. These ties were not easily broken.   Except for his half- brother Linton, and Robert Toombs, Stephen's closest friend had been Abraham Lincoln, who wrote confidentially to Stephens after his election to the presidency in 1860.   Stephens felt called upon to battle against the Confederacy during the war for the same reasons he had fought against the Northern Black Republicans.   Lincoln faced no small battle against many segments of the North, and in his own party, and, whoever the powers behind his assassination were, it seems clear that they were not Southern.   Both in the North and in the South, many favored slavery and many opposed slavery. Again, in both North and South, States' Rights were often opposed, a matter which caused no small controversy in the Confederacy.   Thus, while politically a War Between the States, it was in a tragic sense, and in its remaining and continuing after-effects, a Civil War.

For Stephens, the basic issue in the Civil War was not slavery but *Centralism,* the steady, insistent attempt to overthrow the Constitution and to substitute for the Federal Union a national unitary state.   The entire strategy of Reconstruction, he felt, only confirmed his analysis that slavery was but the occasion chosen for an assault on federalism.   On this presupposition, Stephens wrote his great analysis of the war, *A Constitutional View of the Late War Between the States,* published in 1868 and 1870 in two volumes.[1]   Stephens was a competent and experienced observer.   A lawyer and a citizen of Georgia, he was a notable member of the House of Representatives, 1843-59, first as a Whig, then as a Democrat.   Although opposing secession, he remained loyal to Georgia and became vice-president of the Confederacy, 1861-65, head of the Confederate mission at the Hampton Roads

---

[1] The London *Saturday Review* later said of the *Constitutional View:* " No contribution to the history of the Civil War of equal value has yet been made, or is likely to be made, unless some one of General Lee's few surviving lieutenants should do for the military history of the struggle what Mr. Stephens has done for its political aspect." Myrta Lockett Avary, editor: *Recollections of Alexander H. Stephens, His Diary Kept when a Prisoner at Fort Warren, Boston Harbour, 1865,* p. 548. New York: Doubleday, Page, 1910.

Conference, February, 1865, where he renewed his ties with
Lincoln, and then, after the war, was a prisoner from May
to October, 1865.   He was elected a U.S. Senator in 1866 but
was refused a seat.   Subsequently, he was again a congressman from 1873-1882, and governor of Georgia in 1883.   As
attorney, politician, devout Christian, and a man of considerable intellectual stature, Stephens had no limited perspective
from which to view events.   From this vantage, his analysis
of the conflict was sharply stated:

> That the War had its origin in *opposing principles,*
> which, in their action upon the *conduct of men,* produced
> the ultimate collision of arms, may be assumed as an
> unquestionable fact.   But the opposing principles which
> produced these results in physical action were of a very
> different character from those assumed in the postulate.
> They lay in the organic Structure of Government of the
> States.   The conflict in principle arose from different
> and opposing ideas as to the nature of what is known
> as the General Government.   The contest was between
> those who held it to be strictly Federal in its character,
> and those who maintained that it was thoroughly Na-
> tional.   It was a strife between the principles of Federa-
> tion, on the one side, and Centralism, or Consolidation,
> on the other.
> Slavery, so called, was but *the question* on which
> these antagonistic principles, which had been in conflict,
> from the beginning, on divers *other questions,* were final-
> ly brought into actual and active collision with each
> other on the field of battle.[2]

The Constitution furthered a *Federal* Union, and federal, according to Dr. Johnson and Noah Webster, then meant a
league or alliance between princes or states for their mutual
aid or defense.[3]   Moreover, men were citizens of the United
States only as they became citizens of a particular state in
the Union.[4]

In 1860, an "Anti-Constitutionalist Party" came into
power, dedicated to principles, which, "if carried out, ultimately lead to the absorption of all power in the Central Government, and end sooner or later in Absolutism or Despotism."

[2] Alexander H. Stephens: *A Constitutional View of the Late War
Between the States its Causes, Character, Conduct and Results,* vol. I, p.
10.   Philadelphia: National Publishing Company, 1868.
    [3] *Ibid.,* I, p. 167.
    [4] *Ibid.,* I, p. 34 See also *Recollections,* p. 312f.

The War was thus a conflict of principles, a battle between Constitutionalism and Centralism.[5] The men of this party, the Republicans, were quickly involved in a struggle for power, each seeking to exercise despotic authority. Stephens called attention to instances of this, citing among other things Seward's boast:

> It was in the full exercise of this despotic power that Mr. Seward boasted, in conversation with Lord Lyons, that he could do what her Majesty, Queen Victoria, could not do. In this conversation with the British Minister, Mr. Lincoln's Secretary of State is reported to have said: "I can touch a bell on my right hand and order the arrest of a citizen of Ohio. I can touch the bell again and order the arrest of a citizen of New York. Can Queen Victoria do as much?" He well knew that she could not, and that no Crowned Head in Europe, not even the Czar of Russia, could do more![6]

In his sensitive study of Stephens, Edmund Wilson, who cannot be accused of conservatism, adds a somber footnote to this comment by Stephens, calling attention to the modern reality:

> One is reminded of the boast attributed to Robert Moses, New York Commissioner of Parks and head of the New York State Power Authority: "I can take your house away from you and arrest you for trespassing if you try to go back to it."[7]

Before continuing with Stephens' critique of Centralism, let us examine his opinions with respect to slavery and the Negro. Stephens defended slavery without any apologies. His position was a clear one: first, "the negro is not equal to the white man," so that, second, "subordination to the superior race" is to the Negro's advantage and "is his natural and normal condition." Third, this subordination exists in slavery and is not to be condemned.[8]

Stephens' position, however, differed markedly from the stereotype opinions usually assigned to pro-slavery men. He

---

[5] *Constitutional View*, II, p. 33. 1870.

[6] *Ibid.*, II, p. 409. Stephens was quoting Seward from Fowler's *Sectional Controversy*, p. 350.

[7] Edmund Wilson: *Patriotic Gore*, p. 416.

[8] Stephens, "The 'Corner-Stone' Address," Athenaeum, Savanah, Georgia, March 21, 1861, in Alexander Johnston and James Albert Woodburn: *American Orations, Studies in American Political History*, vol. 4, p. 45. New York: G. P. Putnam's Sons, 1901.

definitely upheld the right of any state or local place to prohibit slavery. This was "not inconsistent with any provision of the Constitution."[9] He denied the right of Nullification, while upholding secession "as a matter of *right*" but opposing it in 1850 and 1860 "as a question of policy."[10]

Stephens believed in Constitutionalism, and "the preservation of the Union upon the principles of the Constitution" was his primary concern.[11] He saw that the consequences of disunion and war would be far more extensive than either Northerners or Southerners recognized; the consequences would be revolution, and "Revolutions are much easier started than controlled, and the men who begin them, even for the best purposes and objects, seldom end them."[12] The "cornerstone" of Constitutionalism for Stephens was not equality but a general "principle of the subordination of the inferior to the superior." This slavery upheld. For Stephens, slavery, while full of evils, was not itself the evil. Education, denied to the slaves, should be supplied, marriages fostered and recognized, and other reforms undertaken.[13] His own status as owner of a few slaves was a good one, and their lot under him an easy one.[14] Stephens did not see slavery as an *economic* fact so much as a *social* fact, not so much one of capital and labor as one of superior and inferior. It was on this

---

[9] Stephens, Letter to the editor of the Federal Union, August 30, 1848, in Annual Report of the American Historical Association, 1911, vol. II, Ulrich B. Phillips, editor: *The Correspondence of Robert Toombs, Alexander H. Stephens, and Howell Cobb*, p. 121, Washington: Government Printing Office, 1913.

[10] Letter to the Public, November 10, 1864, in Phillips, p. 654f.

[11] Letter to Messrs. Fisher and De Leon, February 25, 1852, in Phillips, p. 284. See *Recollections*, p. 146ff., 165ff., 328, for Stephens' emphatic statement that his loyalty was at all times to the Constitution, not to the Union. This loyalty to law was the basis of his disloyalty also to the Confederacy.

[12] Letter to _____, November 25, 1860, in Phillips, p. 504.

[13] *Recollections*, p. 174.

[14] In prison, Stephens could honestly write, in reviewing his life, of his charity to white and Negro:

> I have aided between thirty and forty young men, poor and indigent or without present means, to get an education; the number I do not exactly recollect. Many of these I took through a regular collegiate course, or offered them the means for such a course. My assistance of this character has not been confined to young men; orphans and indigent girls have received liberally of my bounty. I have spent many thousands of dollars

basis that he operated both as slave-owner and thinker.[15]   He recognized very early that the war, however it ended, would not "leave slavery as it found it." Yet the problem of the general relation of superior and inferior, and specifically the racial problem of white and Negro, would remain. "But if the principles of President Lincoln's Emancipation Proclamation—the ultimate policy therein indicated of attempting to establish perfect political and social equality between the races—should be carried out to its final results, it would end in the extermination or the driving from the country of one or the other of the races."[16] With the abolition of slavery, he felt the wisest course was for the slave-holder to take the lead in working to the future interest of the Negro as well as his own.[17]   He wrote in his prison diary with dismay of the bloody riots in Washington, D.C., between soldiers and negroes. The new order of things, by offering equality, was preparing the way for great social conflict. "Sad forebodings haunt me."[18]   Equality would not work.

> How society is to be constituted so that all can attain justice; that is the vexed question. While I confess myself unable to see how it is to be perfectly done, I am equally well satisfied how, in some particulars, it cannot be done, for instance, by any such dogma (not well understood by its advocates) as that all members of society are equal, for this settles nothing.
>
> Equal in what? In age? Facts answer, "No." In feature and appearance? Facts answer, "No." In bodily size or strength? Facts answer, "No." In mental strength or vigour? Facts answer, "No." In moral qualities? Facts answer, "No." In acquirements or accumulations? Facts continue to answer, "No." In not a single one of these particulars can any two amongst millions be found with the dogma of equality. In what

---

for the accommodation and comfort of those recognized as my slaves by our law, over and above all returns they ever made to me. This was of my own earnings. *Recollections*, p. 226f.

It should be remembered that Stephens had been a poor young man who gained his education by debt and was at best later of modest means, himself frail, only 5'-7" and about 96 lbs. in weight, and sickly. Stephens had hoped to reform slave laws with respect to manumission, so that capable slaves might be freed.

[15] *Ibid.*, p. 198f.
[16] *Ibid.*, p. 249f.
[17] *Ibid.*, p. 254.
[18] *Ibid.*, p. 207f.

then are all men by nature equal, or in what ought they to be held to be equal? Is the dogma utterly false and absurd, or is there in it a latent truth which some superficial and rash spirits, nor perceiving, ignore in their misapplication, thus disgusting sincere inquirers?

The dogmatists must admit that all men are not equal in any of the particulars here stated. When asked in what way they are equal or ought to be recognized as equal, one dogmatist will reply one thing and one another, hardly any two agreeing. This shows the vague ideas entertained on the subject. One will say, equal in the eyes of law; another, equal before the law; another, equal in all political rights; another, in all political and social rights. Now, that all men are not equal in the eye of the law is apparent from the fact that the law properly pronounces many persons morally disqualified for membership in society. That all are not and should not be equal in political rights, is apparent from the fact that some must, for the time at least, govern, administer, and execute the law while the rest obey. Between these there is no equality in political power or rights. The right to govern and punish is entirely political; it is not personal or individual. It is impossible, therefore, for all men to be recognized as having equal political rights. What is meant by social rights is too vague and uncertain to define.[19]

Not equality but *justice* should govern the political or moral order and should be the controlling principle. Stephens' definition of this justice was, in common with that of many of the theologians of the day, humanistic,[20] although Stephens himself was a devout Christian who often began his day with a hymn and ended it always with Bible reading and prayer.[21]

The South was governed, Stephens held, by a concern for Constitutionalism, not, as commonly charged, by a "slave oligarchy." Only in South Carolina did the slaveholders hold the political power. The anti-slavery elements in Virginia and North Carolina were strong, and, but for outside agita-

---

[19] *Ibid.*, p. 157f.

[20] *Ibid.*, p. 158-161.

[21] *Ibid.*, pp. 152, 163, 262, 487. Stephens spoke little of his faith, having "a very deep aversion" to "cant," p. 153; he had a lawyer's low opinion of the clergy in relation to civil procedure, p. 311f. He was, while very devout, not too discriminating in theological matters, p. 470, 472f. With respect to the religious and social background of the South, Stephens denied that it was Cavalier rather than Puritan, except possibly for Virginia, p. 420ff.

tion, internal forces would have abolished slavery. In general, however, the Georgia situation best described the South, perhaps, where only a minority were slaveholders. In Georgia, Stephens held, "eight-tenths" would have abolished slavery "if they could have seen what better they could do with the coloured people than they were doing."[22]

With the end of the war, the misrepresentation of the South began in full force. Stephens observed, from prison:

> I went to the library and got Richardson's new book "The Secret Service, The Field, The Dungeon and The Escape." I doubt the author's accuracy. I doubt if he saw Negro women in raw hide shoes ploughing in Kentucky in February, which is too early for ploughing. Rawhide shoes I never saw anywhere. I heard that they were used by our soldiers to some extent, being made and fitted to the foot when the hide was fresh and green, with the hairside next the foot. How a man could see the kind of leather shoes were made of, worn by workers ploughing in a field which he was passing on a railroad train, I cannot understand. Then again, he speaks of seeing Negroes ploughing and hoeing in fields near Memphis. Now, what were they *hoeing?* *Hoeing* is a business not done in cotton-fields, and of such he is speaking in February. Overseers were there, armed with guns. This I never saw in all my life and in all my travels through the South. I have sometimes seen a man, superintending plantations, carry his gun with the view of bagging game, but never for any purpose in connection with his business as overseer. These are all small matters. But my rule with a record is to judge its accuracy as a whole by accuracy on those points within my knowledge.[23]

Before the war, Stephens had tried to stem Southern fears regarding his friend Lincoln, whom he declared to be "just as good, safe and sound a man as Mr. Buchanan," and one who "would administer the Government so far as he is individually concerned just as safely for the South and

---

[22] *Ibid.,* p. 422. The war did not diminish Southern anti-slavery feeling. Because slaves were not subject to the regulations and conscription imposed on the citizenry, they were in a sense privileged. Exemption from military service was allowed under conscription for one white man as overseer for every twenty slaves whose work required supervision. Thus the whole slave system was a privileged order resented by many, and the great majority were not slaveholders.

[23] *Ibid.,* p. 440.

as honestly and faithfully *in every particular.*" The South's greatest security was *in* the Union, and the best security for the Union was *peace.* "We have nothing to fear from anything so much as unnecessary changes and revolutions in government. The institution is *based* on conservatism. Everything that weakens this has a tendency to weaken the institution."[24] In spite of his respect for and confidence in Lincoln, he knew what the success of Republicanism would mean to the South. Hence, "My greatest desire is to defeat Lincoln and thus prevent the evils that such an event might precipitate upon us."[25]

In his speech to the Georgia Legislature, November 14, 1860, against secession, Stephens called attention to the fact that the victorious Republicans had won an election but had not gained control of Congress. Lincoln did not share all his party's views, but assuming he did, the House had a large majority against the Republicans. Indeed, the anti-abolitionist and anti-centralist position had made notable gains in the House in Northern states. In the Senate, Lincoln faced a majority of four against him. "Why then I say, should we disrupt the ties of this union, when his hands are tied—when he can do nothing against us?"[26] Very many responsible Southerners shared this view. Stephens further charged that "sectionalism" was subverting Constitutionalism, and the guilt of the South here was no less than that of the North. Whatever the provocation, "I give it to you as my opinion, that but for the policy the Southern people pursued, this fearful result would not have occurred."[27] For Stephens, "The doctrine of the 'Irrespressible Conflict' between the Institutions of the several States, was, in my view, itself the embodiment of Centralism. The Federal Government, in my judgment, so far from being weakened, was strengthened by the heterogeneous interest of the several States. Nothing tends more to Centralization of power, even in a separate State or Nation, than homogeneousness of interests on the part of its constituent elements."[28] Here we see a basic premise of Stephens' political theory. Since a society is not

---

[24] Letter to J. Henley Smith, July 10, 1860, in Phillips, p. 487.
[25] Letter to J. Henley Smith, September 12, 1860, *ibid.,* p. 496.
[26] *Constitutional View,* II, p. 282f.
[27] *Ibid.,* II, 280.
[28] *Ibid.,* II, 309.

a final product, an end-of-history order, it must be a working, struggling body. To decry necessary conflict, as many in the North and South were doing, was to decry in effect, history itself, or, as Stephens worded it, constitutionalism in favor of Centralism and homogeneity. Stephens knew that constitutionalism was being challenged, even as it had been challenged in the past and would be again in the future. History means struggle. To attempt to evade this fact of struggle by seeking a homogeneous society in flight can mean the necessity of repeated flight. For Stephens, the best hope for constitutionalism, and for the South, was for a stand to be made *in* the Union. Through the conflict of ideas and parties, with the confrontation of basic issues, the Union could be strengthened, and greater health could ensue. But the South failed to see this, and the Confederacy was born. Stephens became its vice-president.

It is not our purpose here to review Stephens' war-time activities. In the North, Lincoln assumed unconstitutional powers to suppress criticism and to further the war effort. In the South, Jefferson Davis reluctantly felt it necessary to move in the same direction, although never so far.[29] Stephens and his friends were already severe critics of the Confederate monetary policy, opposing deficit operation in favor of heavy taxation.[30] Moreover, according to Toombs, "We never had a desertion until we had conscription, for the very good reason that there were thousands outside who wanted to take the places of those inside." With conscription, deterioration of morale and unwillingness to serve set in. "When we began to hunt up men with dogs like the Mexicans, they necessarily became as worthless as Mexicans, and every day has seen the deterioration of troops in as conscripts."[31] Toombs also charged that the independent press was largely bought up and silenced.[32] It can be freely granted that the criticisms of Stephens, Joseph E. Brown, Governor of Georgia, as well

---

[29] See Jefferson Davis' message to the confederate Senate and House, December 7, 1863, in James D. Richardson: *A Compilation of the Messages and Papers of the Confederacy*, vol. I, pp. 345-382. Nashville: U. S. Publishing Co., 1905.

[30] Robert Toombs, Letter to the Editor of the Augusta, Georgia, *Constitutionalist*, August 12, 1863, in Phillips, p. 622ff.

[31] Robert Toombs, Letter to W. W. Burwell, August 20, 1863, in Phillips, p. 629.

[32] Toombs, Letter to Stephens, April 1, 1864, in Phillips, p. 636-639.

as of others were often intemperate and unfair, but their basic premise remains unexamined, and these men in turn are now subjected to abuse by historians. Stephens has been accused of "narrowness, pettiness, and lack of realism" by Potter.[33] Another writer has charged Stephens, in his hopes of peace and restoration to the Union, with a serious responsibility for the collapse of the Confederacy.[34] The presupposition to these usually liberal critics is best stated by Donald:

> The collapse of the Confederacy, then, came not from deficient economic resources, insufficient manpower, defective strategy, or weak political leadership. All of these were handicaps; but none was fatal. The real weakness of the Confederacy was that the Southern people insisted upon retaining their democratic liberties in wartime. If they were fighting for freedom, they asked, why should they start abridging it? As soldiers, as critics of their government, and as voters they stuck to their democratic, individualistic rights. In the administration of the Southern army, in the management of Southern civilian affairs, and in the conduct of Southern political life, there is, then, extensive evidence that we should write on the tombstone of the Confederacy: "Died of Democracy."[35]

This is the issue. There was no lack of willingness on the part of these Southerners like Stephens to sacrifice except at one point: they were unwilling to sacrifice their constitutional liberties. Are the modern critics right? Is it necessary, in war-time, for a state to become totalitarian? Is this the price of efficiency and of direction? Certainly, half-way measures, such as the South took, halt between two opinions and have none of the virtues of either position, but the case for liberty is not being examined, even though in World War II, the success of American free enterprise in meeting the war-time demands placed upon it depended to a large degree on its successful circumvention of government controls. The black market was a major contributor to efficiency and to victory. The demands for war-time controls that have arisen increasingly with each war are parallel to the growing con-

---

[33] David M. Potter, "Jefferson Davis and the Political Factors in Confederate Defeat," in David Donald, ed.: *Why the North Won the Civil War*, p. 100. New York: Collier, 1962.

[34] Rudolph von Abele: *Alexander H. Stephens, A Biography*, p. 254f. New York: Knopf, 1946.

[35] David Donald, "Died of Democracy" in Donald, p. 90.

ception and use of *war as revolution*. This having become an ever-increasing function of war, it has become increasingly important to insist on the *sacrifice of liberty* as the foremost requirement of the art of war. Stephens was aware that war could mean revolution, and he fought the Confederacy's policies in the name of Constitutionalism, the same cause he had championed in the Union. As Stephens had always made clear, his loyalty was not to the Federal Government, nor to the South, but to the Constitution, which the South had also adopted with adaptations. The Centralism Stephens fought in Washington, he also fought in Richmond.

Again, for Stephens Centralism was the premise of the Radical Republican Reconstruction, which he criticized, "the Monster Principle of *ultimate* complete Centralism."[36]   The purpose of the Centralists, "their *ultimate* object," he saw as "Consolidation and Empire."[37]   The Negro was a pawn in the game, who would gain only a ghetto status. In prison, he hoped that the South would spike this strategy by taking the lead in Negro welfare. He suggested that Negroes be given a corporate or guild status with proportionate representation from and in each state to have a full, free and separate representation.[38]   In his sleep in prison, he dreamed of home, and of instructing his ex-slaves in the meaning of liberty, and woke up, "my eyes streaming with tears."[39]   He was horrified at the abuse of Negroes that multiplied across the country outside the South: "Mrs. Stowe ought to write another book. The Legrees are multiplying fast all around."[40] He saw no hope for the South or the Union under Reconstruction.[41] He felt that Johnson, whom he respected, was "committing a great error in bringing into prominence the secession

---

[36] *Constitutional View*, II, p. 639.

[37] *Ibid.*, II, p. 649f.

[38] *Recollections*, pp. 267-274. He suggested this plan to Seward by letter offering to write further on it, pp. 371-375. On his release from prison, he discussed it with President Johnson, but it was then "too late" to consider such a change, p. 53f: see also p. 544-546. Stephens felt that much trouble would have been avoided by Southerners after the war by "allowing a wisely-restricted suffrage to the black race in their new constitutions," p. 546.

[39] *Ibid.*, p. 315.

[40] *Ibid.*, p. 318.

[41] *Ibid.*, p. 350f.

element at the South instead of the original Union element."[42]
As he looked to the future, Stephens was deeply troubled:

> The great vital question now is: Shall the Federal Gov-
> ernment be arrested in its progress, and be brought back
> to original principles, or shall it be permitted to go on
> in its present tendencies and rapid strides, until it reaches
> complete Consolidation!
>
> Depend upon it, there is no difference between Con-
> solidation and Empire; no difference between Centralism
> and Imperialism. The consummation of either must
> necessarily end in the overthrow of Liberty and the estab-
> lishment of Despotism. To speak of any Rights as be-
> longing to the States, without the innate and unalienated
> Sovereign power to maintain them, is but to deal in the
> shadow of language without the substance. Nominal
> Rights without Securities are but Mockeries![43]

As Toombs wrote to Stephens, the Democrats were now
in the hands of a "mongrel crew" and would rather worship
Beelzebub than God but preferred "Mammon to either if they
could perchance reach the treasury."[44]   The Union's monetary
policy was a vast swindle.[45]   With all this, Stephens sadly
agreed.   In 1881, two years before his death, he summarized
his views thus:

> If ever there is another war in this republic, it will
> not be sectional, but social. . .   If ever the masses of the
> people can be made to understand our system of class-
> legislation, taxes and finance, there will be trenchant
> reform or frightful revolution.[46]

The years have only underscored the relevancy of Stephens' analysis.   From a very limited system of privately owned slaves, the entire United States has, from the Civil War
era, gone into debt-money slavery to the "Money Trust," so
that its very monetary wealth, being debt-money, is itself a
sign of bondage.

---

[42] *Ibid.*, p. 515.

[43] *Constitutional View*, II, p. 668.   See also Stephens: *History of
the United States*, p. 915, Du Lac, Wisconsin: Benjamin, 1882.

[44] Robert Toombs, Letter to Stephens, October 30, 1876, in Phillips,
p. 722.

[45] Robert Toombs, Letter to Stephens, January 25, 1878, in Phillips,
p. 732ff.

[46] Rudolph von Abele: *Stephens*, p. 304.

CHAPTER IV

THE ATTACK ON RELIGIOUS LIBERTY

Historically, there are two major stages in the attack on religious liberty. First, the state is secularized in the name of freedom, and, second, every prerogative of the church is attacked in an indirect manner so that, in disguised fashion, its right to exist is denied. The word *tyrant,* from the Greek *tyranos,* means a secular ruler, one who rules without the sanction of religious law, with "an authority that was not derived from the worship, a power that religion had not established." Its new principle of law was *democracy,* "the obedience of man to man." "It is a general fact, and almost without exception in the history of Greece and of Italy, that the tyrants sprang from the popular party, and had the aristocracy as enemies." Moreover, "the tyrant always made war upon the rich."[1] Instead of a higher law, the tyrant sees his mandate in the will of the people, vox populi, vox dei. *Right* is what the people want. Tyranny is thus inevitably in conflict with religion because it cannot tolerate a law which denies that the people are the source of law, which asserts that there is a divine order which stands in judgment over the human order. By affirming as his principle "The People, Yes," the tyrant must sooner or later logically affirm its corollary by saying to God an emphatic *no.* And, however servile the churches and clergy may be, and however subversive of their faith, they must still be undermined, the very idea of religion, (probably from the Latin word *religare,* to hold back, to bind fast; *ligare,* to bind) means that the binding power between tyrant and people resides elsewhere than in his incarnation of the general will of the people.

---

[1] Fustel de Coulanges: *The Ancient City,* pp. 271, 342. Garden City; Doubleday Anchor Books, 1956.

The United States, in its inception as a constitutional government, was not a secular state.   As we have noted, it abstained from any particular form of Christian settlement because this was the prerogative of the states.   Each of the constituent states was a Christian republic, and the federal government was restricted from making any laws interfering with their settlements.   But the federal government was not secular.   Indeed, not until the French Revolution introduced the concept did any state in the western world contemplate the possibility of being a secular or non-Christian order.   In a multitude of provisions placing the sanction of the faith upon its activities, and by the oath of office, then an important religious act, the federal government made clear its Christian nature.[2]

Every state, including the United States, was immediately challenged by the French Revolution.   The Enlightenment dream of reason was here translated into a walking nightmare, and this new French state, grounded on reason rather than the law of God, became at once the heavenly and the earthly city of the anti-Christian and deistic forces of the day. Academic discussions and table talk now become potent subversive political forces.   The shock of this new movement was felt by every western order, and in the United States George Washington directed his Farewell Address to a consideration of it.

Issued on September 17, 1796, Washington's Farewell Address cannot be understood except in terms of his deep concern over the events in Europe.   For diplomatic reasons, France and its revolution are not named, but the basic ideas are dealt with.   Washington struck out sharply at the idea of the secular state, at the idea that there could be a separation of religion and political order, and of religion and morality.

> Of all the dispositions and habits, which lead to political prosperity, religion and morality are indispensable supports.   In vain would that man claim the tribute of patriotism, who should labor to subvert these great pillars of human happiness, these firmest props of the duties of men and citizens.   The mere politician, equally with the pious man, ought to respect and to cherish them.   A volume could not trace all their connexions with private

[2] This writer is indebted to Michael D. Stingley for his insights, in an as yet unfinished study, of the nature of the oath in the early years of the United States.

and public felicity. Let it simply be asked, Where is the security for property, for reputation, for life, if the sense of religious obligation desert the oaths, which are the instruments of investigation in courts of justice? And let us with caution indulge the supposition, that morality can be maintained without religion. Whatever may be conceded to the influence of refined education on minds of peculiar structure, reason and experience both forbid us to expect, that national morality can prevail in exclusion of religious principle.

It is substantially true, that virtue or morality is a necessary spring of popular government. The Rule, indeed, extends with more or less force to every species of free government. Who, that is a sincere friend to it, can look with indifference upon attempts to shake the foundation of the fabric?

"The foundation of the fabric" was for Washington the necessary connection between religion and morality. Washington's theological orientation is not our concern here, but his insistence on the primacy of the religious or theological issue is.

As Washington saw it, the state is a form of moral order, and moral order rests on religion. Morality cannot be maintained without religion. "The security for property, for reputation, for life," and the very courts of justice, are gone when *moral order* is divorced from religion, *theological order*. What will happen if men look to reason rather than to religion for law? Men may perhaps agree *generally* that "Thou shalt not steal" is a necessary law for social order, but they will not agree as readily to defining theft *specifically*. Is confiscatory taxation directed at the rich social justice, or is it immorality? Is inflation moral, or is it theft? Is private property itself a moral order, or is it a form of theft? In a "rational" order, the "reason" of the majority, or of a democratic elite, will prevail, and morality will change as that controlling group changes. Instead of fixed moral order law will follow the election returns or the will of the Establishment. Moral order apart from theological order is an illusion productive only of anarchy and decay. Indeed, "reason and experience both forbid us to expect, that national morality can prevail in exclusion of religious principle," i.e., theological order. Washington's opposition to the secular state was thus clear-cut: it spelled the destruction of liberty, and of all free civil government, "to every species of free government."

Forces for secularization were present in Washington's day and later, French sympathizers and Jacobins, deists, Illuminati, Freemasons, and soon the Unitarians. But the legal steps towards secularization were only taken in the 1950's and 1960's by the U. S. Supreme Court. For the sake of argument, we may concede to the liberal, and to some orthodox Christian scholars, that Deism had made extensive inroads into America by 1776, and 1787, and that the men of the Constitutional Convention, and Washington, were influenced by it. The fact still remains that they did not attempt to create a secular state. The states were Christian states, and the federal union, while barred from intervention in this area, was not itself secular. The citizens were citizens of their respective states and of the United States simultaneously. They could not be under two sets of religious law. Officers of the federal government, president and congress, worshiped as an official body, but without preference extended to a single church. The chaplaincy, oaths of office, the legal fact of the church as a separate law sphere, these and other things pointed to the acceptance of religious order as the foundation of moral and political order. Secularism asserts the self-sufficiency or self-containment of the moral and political order. Certainly, Arminianism and Deism prepared the ground for the acceptance of such a concept, so that the seeds of secularism were present in colonial America. The constitutional system, however, was not the product of these seeds, but of very concrete and long standing realities. The Constitution was the capstone of the Protestant feudal restoration; the religious and political foundation lay far below it. The U. S. Supreme Court, in nullifying various religious practices in the states, has not struck out at novelties on the American scene but at the legal situation as it has existed from the beginning of the United States to the present. Not until 1940, long after the Fourteenth Amendment (1868) was added to the Constitution, did the U. S. Supreme Court "restrict State action respecting religion." At that time, "without any change in the Constitution, it was held that the Constitution in this regard meant precisely the reverse of what it had meant for the first 152 years of its existence."[3]

---

[3] Virginia Commission on Constitutional Government: *The New York Prayer Case*, p. 7. Richmond, Virginia, 1962.

The change came, but it was slow in coming. There was good reason for this delay, in spite of the intensity of this drive towards secularism. As Singer has observed,

> A Christian world and life view furnished the basis for this early political thought which guided the American people for nearly two centuries and whose crowning lay in the writing of the Constitution of 1787. This Christian theism had so permeated the colonial mind that it continued to guide even those who had come to regard the Gospel with indifference or even hostility. The currents of this orthodoxy were too strong to be easily set aside by those who in their own thinking had come to a different conception of religion and hence of government also.[4]

Moreover, while Calvinism had receded in New England by 1787, it was coming into new power in the central states and in the South. And, when Princeton Seminary was a lonely bastion of Calvinism in the North, that faith held sway in the South. Indeed, an important aspect of the Civil War was the Unitarian statist drive for an assault on its Calvinistic enemy, the South. In 1828-32, many Southern conservatives had refused to support South Carolina and Calhoun in the nullification controversy because of the liberal theological orientation of its leaders. Thomas Cooper, president of the University of South Carolina, a major champion of nullification, was a noted Deist and Unitarian. Unitarianism, however, quickly oriented itself to abolitionism, and the South, itself concerned about slavery, came to defend itself against the revolutionary principles which were being applied against it. One of the greatest of the Southern Presbyterian Calvinists, Benjamin M. Palmer, in his "Thanksgiving Sermon" of November 29, 1860, in New Orleans, took as his texts Psalm 94:20: "Shall the throne of iniquity have fellowship with thee, which frameth mischief by a law?" and Obadiah 7: "All the men of thy confederacy have brought thee even to the border; the men that were at peace with thee have deceived thee, and prevailed against thee; they that ate thy bread have laid a wound under thee: there is none understanding in him." The gathering conflict (South Carolina had moved as early as November 17, 1860) Palmer saw as the forces of false theology, of

---

[4] C. Gregg Singer: *A Theological Interpretation of American History*, p. 284f. Nutley, N.J., Craig Press, 1964.

atheism and of the French Revolution, of the religion of humanity in short, arrayed against a Christian people dedicated to faith in Jesus Christ as Lord and Savior, and to Constitutional government. These forces sought to frame "mischief by a law." The South had slavery; the North had its growing and fearful problems of capital versus labor. Interference by the one into the problems of the other could not be tolerated, because it would be destructive of social order. Moreover, "In the imperfect state of human society, it pleases God to allow evils which check others that are greater." The anti-Christian, Jacobin attack on slavery had to be fought, and slavery defended, because the revolutionary re-ordering of society would be far worse than anything it sought to supplant. "Human legislation" was seeking to supplant God and to set "bounds to what God can alone regulate." "The country is convulsed simply because 'the throne of iniquity frameth mischief by a law.'" In a remarkable paragraph, Palmer summarized the basic issue very bluntly:

> Last of all, in this great struggle, we defend the cause of God and religion. The abolition spirit is undeniably atheistic. The demon which erected its throne upon the guillotine in the days of Robespierre and Marat, which abolished the Sabbath and worshipped reason in the person of a harlot, yet survives to work other horrors, of which those of the French Revolution are but the type. Among a people so generally religious as the American, a disguise must be worn; but it is the same old threadbare disguise of the advocacy of human rights. From a thousand Jacobin clubs here, as in France, the decree has gone forth which strikes at God by striking at all subordination and law. Availing itself of the morbid and misdirected sympathies of men, it has entrapped weak consciences in the meshes of its treachery; and now, at last, has seated its high priest upon the throne, clad in the black garments of discord and schism, so symbolic of its ends. Under this suspicious cry of reform, it demands that every evil shall be corrected, or society become a wreck—the sun must be stricken from the heavens, if a spot is found upon his disk. The Most High, knowing his own power, which is infinite, and his own wisdom, which is unfathomable, can afford to be patient. But these self-constituted reformers must quicken the activity of Jehovah or compel his abdication. In their furious haste, they trample upon obligations sacred as any which can bind the conscience. It is time to reproduce the obsolete

THE ATTACK ON RELIGIOUS LIBERTY   51

idea that Providence must govern man, and not that man
shall control Providence. In the imperfect state of
human society, it pleases God to allow evils which check
others that are greater. As in the physical world, objects are moved forward, not by a single force, but by the
composition of forces; so in his moral administration,
there are checks and balances whose intimate relations
are comprehended only by himself. But what reck they
of this—these fierce zealots who undertake to drive the
chariot of the sun? Working out the single and false
idea which rides them like a nightmare, they dash
athwart the spheres, utterly disregarding the delicate
mechanism of Providence, which moves on, wheels within
wheels, with pivots and balances and springs, which the
great Designer alone can control. This spirit of atheism,
which knows no God who tolerates evil, no Bible which
sanctions law, and no conscience that can be bound by
oaths and covenants, has selected us for its victims, and
slavery for its issue. Its banner-cry rings out already
upon the air—'liberty, equality, fraternity,' which simply
interpreted mean bondage, confiscation and massacre.
With its tricolor waving in the breeze,—it waits to inaug-
urate its reign of terror. To the South the high position
is assigned of defending, before all nations, the cause of
all religion and of all truth. In this trust, we are resist-
ing the power which wars against constitutions and laws
and compacts, against Sabbaths and sanctuaries, against
the family, the State, and the Church; which blasphem-
ously invades the prerogatives of God, and rebukes the
Most High for the errors of his administration; which, if
it cannot snatch the reign of empires from his grasp, will
lay the universe in ruins at his feet. Is it possible that we
shall decline the onset?[5]

This attention to Palmer may seem at first glance merely
an interesting digression from the question of secularization,
but certainly Palmer felt that secularization was the issue.
The United States in that day was definitely Christian. Calvinism had lost ground to Arminian revivalism in the North
and West, but it commanded much of the South. It was necessary, therefore, to disguise the secularization with ostensibly
Christian idealism. "Among a people so generally religious
as the American, a disguise must be worn; but it is the same
old threadbare disguise of the advocacy of human rights." It

[5] Thomas Cary Johnson: *The Life and Letters of Benjamin Morgan
Palmer* p. 212f. Richmond, Va.: Presbyterian Committee of Publication,
1906.

was the assertion of the primacy of moral order to theological order, and an insistence sometimes of the independence of the moral order. It was what Washington termed it, "the supposition, that morality can be maintained without religion." It was, moreover, the belief that no religion could dare exist if any evil continued: "Under this suspicious cry of reform, it demands that every evil shall be corrected, or society become a wreck—the sun must be stricken from the heavens, if a spot is found upon his disk." The religion of humanity disguised itself in terms calculated to arouse the simple evangelical adherents of the religion of Jesus Christ to a feeling of guilt unless certain political goals could be attained. Both church and state were to be secularized by the disguised promulgation of secular goals and secular laws. The "social gospel" made men feel steadily that the "theological gospel" was irrelevant and trivial. It was insisted that it was silly and irreverent to insist on strict trinitariansm, and on the divine institution or ordination of civil government and man's duty to recognize and obey authorities, when *man* was in need. The pre-eminent fact was not the satisfaction of the justice of God in the atoning sacrifice of Jesus Christ, and the law orders attendant upon that fact, but it was instead the satisfaction of man.

Thus, from the Civil War to World War II, the goals of the state were secularized and nationalized. The purposes of law became increasingly not the reflection of God's justice, without respect of persons, but social justice, the triumph of humanism. After World War II, the United States saw the steady internationalization of its religion of humanity, and at the same time, attention finally to the *legal* secularization of the states. With the rising tide of conservatism, both economic and political, and then the steady association of this with the revival of Christian orthodoxy, the legal possibility of exploiting the long-latent potentialities of a Christian society had to be nullified.

In 1954, the Pledge of Allegiance had added to it two words: "one nation *under God,* indivisible, with liberty and justice for all" by act of Congress. At about the same time the U. S. Supreme Court commented, "We are a religious people whose institutions presuppose a Supreme Being" (*Zorach* v. *Clauson*, 343 U.S. 306, 313).

Carefully nurtured, planned, and financed test cases were already under way, and the matter built up to the New York

Prayer Case, June 25, 1962.   The outcry over this case exceeded previous decisions because the extent of conservative resistance was now greater.   "A heavy volume of mail" reached the U. S. Supreme Court, "almost none of it complimentary."   Extensive editorial comment also indicated the general dismay at the decision.[6]   It was widely recognized that the U. S. Supreme Court had changed the law, that it had reversed longstanding and fully legal practices.   As even one temporizing newspaperman wrote, with reference to the first amendment,

> At the time of its adoption, nine of the thirteen states had established churches.   Some legislators voted for the amendment in the belief that it would prevent the new federal government from interfering with these state "establishments of religion."   Others had precisely the opposite intent.   Thomas Jefferson, in a private letter, construed the amendment as erecting "a wall of separation between church and state."   Many, then as now, took it to mean what James Madison said in his first draft: "The civil rights of none shall be abridged on account of religious beliefs or worship, nor shall any national religion be established."[7]

It was obvious even to such writers, even as they tried to moderate the facts, that radical changes had been introduced. Neither the nine states, nor any of the others, had any expec-

---

[6] See *The Presbyterian Journal*, July 10, 1963, vol. XXII, no. 11, p. 4. " 'Devotional' Decision Starts Flood of Mail"; *Life*, vol. 54, no. 11, March 15, 1963, p. 4, Editorial "The Bible—Better in School Than in Court"; *Oakland (Calif.) Tribune*, Sunday, July 28, 1963, p. 31, Editorial, "Walling Out God"; *San Francisco Examiner*, Sunday, August 18, 1963, p. 1f., Editor's Report, "Bring God Back to Our Schools," by William Randolph Hearst, Jr.; *San Francisco Examiner*, Thursday, July 11, 1963, pp. 1, 17, "Cardinal Denounces Court on Prayer."   For Catherine Machin's "The Court's Changing Views on Religion in Schools," see also the S. F. Examiner, Sunday, June 23, 1963, Sec. I, p. 9.   For the legal status and extent of use of the Bible in schools at an earlier date, see Wilbur F. Crafts: *Bible in Schools Plans of Many Lands*, Washington, D. C.:   Illustrated Bible Selections Commission, 1914. See also W. S. Fleming: *God in Our Public Schools*, Pittsburgh: National Reform Association, 1942. See also "Outlawing God," *The Dan Smoot Report*, vol. 10, no. 9, March 2, 1964; *Don Bell Reports*, Year ten, nos. 1, 24, January 4, June 21, 1963.

[7] Louis Cassels, "Is God Unconstitutional?   Barring Official Prayers Might Shock Foundling Fathers Who Were Religious." in *Palo Alto (Calif.) Times*, Saturday, July 14, 1962, p. 26.

tation whatsoever, when the first amendment was ratified, that it would do more than bar *Congress* from interference in religious matters, and not a single state practice then or later was modified because of it. Cassels stated the point of the decision, however: mandatory neutrality was implied.

> If this constitutional philosophy is carried to its logical conclusion, as Justices William O. Douglas and Potter Stewart said in their opinions in the prayer case, it would seem to prohibit tax exemptions to churches and many other long-established government practices.[8]

Cases were started to prohibit tax exemption to churches, to abolish "under God" from the Pledge of Allegiance, and "In God We Trust" from public documents and from money. The American Civil Liberties Union was active in such matters.[9]

In spite of the storm of protest, all kinds of steps to further secularization were immediately taken. Christmas carols and nativity scenes in schools were barred. Chief Justice Earl Warren of the U. S. Supreme Court was hostile to the inscription of "In God We Trust" on the Supreme Court Building.[10] Examples of the extent to which legal use was made of the new ruling can be cited from Santa Monica, California. Public Works Director Bartlett L. Kennedy asked City Attorney Robert G. Cockins to rule, first, on the distribution of religious literature in boxes at Palisades Park, and, second, on the annual Christmas Nativity scenes there. "Kennedy promptly forbade further distribution of the matter in the park," with a ruling on the Nativity scenes promised early the next week. "A wave of protests" compelled the city council to rescind the ban, but the Mayor, Rex Minter, attempted to dismiss the issue as "a tempest in a teapot," to

---

[8] *Idem.*

[9] *Oakland (Calif.) Tribune*, Editorials, Friday, March 29, 1963, p. 27, "The Strange ACLU Mentality," and Friday, June 21, 1963, p. 23, "A Weak Case." See also *S. F. Examiner*, Sunday, July 1, 1962, Section II, p. 1, Dick Nolan, "The City." On the ACLU, see *Does The American Civil Liberties Union Serve the Communist Cause?*, Fact Committee, P.O. Box 1724, Phoenix 1, Arizona.

[10] *The Presbyterian Journal*, November 27, 1963, vol. XXII, no. 31, p 3f., "Court, Congress Fight Over 'In God We Trust';" see also Robert S. Allen and Paul Scott, "Washington Report: A Slow Decision on Inscription," *Oakland (Calif.) Tribune*, Monday, December 11, 1962, p. 11.

which the Rev. A. J. Edwards, Church of the Nazarene, made emphatic denial.[11]

However, as one writer observed, the major battle between "Religion and Rights" is "yet to break."[12]

As indicated earlier, the first stage of the attack on religious liberty is the secularization of the state in the name of freedom. This secularization is both philosophical and legal. The meaning and goals of the state are secularized, and then, its life being now secular, its laws are divorced from Christian faith.

In the second stage of the attack, the prerogatives and liberty of the church are attacked, in an indirect and disguised fashion, so that gradually its very right to exist is denied. No attempt will be made here to give a full account of these attacks: only to indicate something of their nature and direction.

Certainly a central thrust in this stage of attack is to remove tax-exemption from the churches. A news story indicates the reality of this factor:

Baltimore, Oct. 16 (AP)—Madelyn Murray, whose suit in the U. S. Supreme Court knocked out required prayer and Bible reading in public schools, has filed another one which challenges tax exemptions for church-owned property.

Mrs. Murray's lawyer filed suit in Superior Court Tuesday asking the court to declare the tax-exemption unconstitutional. Her argument is that the exemption places a financial burden on her.

Furthermore, she says, the practice denies taxpayers due process of law under the 14th Amendment, and it violates the principle of church-state separation. The suit contends that property taxes for individuals would be reduced by 1 to 5 per cent if the churches are made to pay.[13]

[11] *Los Angeles Herald-Examiner*, Sunday, October 27, 1963, p. CCC 5, "They May Ban Nativity Scene," and Thursday, October 31, 1963, p. A-14, "Santa Monica Kills Religious Books Ban."

[12] *Palo Alto (Calif.) Times*, Wednesday, August 22, 1962, p. 22, Claire Cox, "Religion and Rights. The Storm is Yet to Break," and Thursday, August 23, 1962, p. 27, "Still More Suits Expected. Volume of Church-State legal cases increases."

[13] *The Washington Post*, Thursday, Oct. 17. 1963, p. D 3.

There are many other things today that place a "financial burden" on Mrs. Murray by means of taxation, but she has no desire to have these things declared unconstitutional.

It would be true, yet beside the point, to defend the tax exemption of churches on the ground that they are non-profit institutions and corporations. The real issue is the liberty of the church. As the U. S. Supreme Court itself noted, early in its history, "the power to tax is the power to destroy." It is as unjust to place the church under the state as it is to place the state under the church. The tax-exemption of the church went hand in hand with the state's abstention from the internal affairs of the churches, their law, government and doctrine, on the ground that church and state constitute two different law spheres, both directly under God rather than under one another. To ask the church to render tribute unto Caesar is to deny that it has any direct approach to God, to declare, in essence, that the church's approach to God and man is mediated through the state. This is precisely the same issue as that involved in emperor worship in the days of the Roman Empire, and in Shinto Shrine worship in the Japanese Empire.

It can be objected that a number of prominent churchmen, and some church groups as well, can be cited in favor of the taxation of churches. The obvious answer is an examination of the records of these persons and groups. They have not distinguished themselves in the defense of Christian orthodoxy. Rather, they have been eloquent champions of the religion of humanity, of a socialized order and a social rather than a theological gospel.

It is futile to "grant" religious liberty if this right over the church be claimed. The U.S.S.R. is ready to affirm a constitutional freedom of worship, but its claim to the control of religion renders this guarantee null and void.

In the days of the Roman Empire, it was the time-serving and heretical clergy who promoted imperial power and saw the emperor as the true representative of God on earth. The orthodox churchmen refused to submit to a subordinationist Christology or to recognize the mediatorial role of the state, and were persecuted for this faith.

If the church pays taxes to the state, it means that the church then exists in the state and by grace of the state, and is a subject or citizen of the state. This the true church can never recognize nor permit. Emperor worship does not become respectable and holy by its transfer from Rome to the United States.

Already, steps are being taken to prepare the way for this renewed emperor worship. It was once sufficient for a church to be in existence and to have purchased or built its property to have its tax exempt status. Inroads are being made on this. One inroad is the *annual* requirement for the filing of tax exempt papers by churches, so that the church must annually confirm its status. The churches are assured that this is a mere formality, but the *requirement* of this mere formality is a requirement of submission. Another planned inroad is a nominal *filing fee* annually for the tax exemption, so that a tax is imposed for tax exemption!

All this is *disguised rather than direct*. It is all the more an insidious attack on religious liberty, and more dangerous, in that few are able to detect its implications and direction.

Another major area of attack is through planning commissions and zoning laws. Zoning laws have an air of progress and civic improvement, and they appeal to the desire of people to improve their property while steadily infringing on their property rights.

As early as the 1940's, the Federal Council of Churches of Christ, together with local councils of churches and the Home Missions Council of North America developed a "Master Plan" for the location and relocation of Protestant churches. Dr. H. Paul Douglass, director of Co-operative Field Research for the F.C.C.C.A., toured the country, conferring with local leaders to set up the plan. Area Comity Councils of cooperating churches were created. The plan for the proper location of churches was then urged on city planning commissions. Very quickly, orthodox church groups outside the F.C.C.C.A. found themselves unable to get permits to build. Thus the Rev. Lawrence R. Eyres had organized the First Orthodox Presbyterian Church in Portland, Oregon, and applied for permission to build on their lots. The answer they received was the following statement: "There are already enough churches of all denominations to serve the needs of this community and it is therefore economically unsound to place additional churches there." When Eyres sought to push the matter,

>Then began a campaign of innuendo and political
wire-pulling which should bring shame to the faces of
people who call themselves Christian. City employees,
when approached about the matter, directed inquirers to
the Portland Council of Churches with the information
that the First Orthodox Presbyterian Church was a "non-
cooperative church." A campaign was begun to get sig-
natures on a petition to City Council urging denial of the
application. Every conceivable argument logical and il-
logical prejudicial to the project was used.[14]

The First Orthodox Presbyterian Church, facing a long legal
battle and declining attendance because of inadequate rented
facilities, bought property outside the city limits, built there,
and prospered.

This was not an isolated instance. Many other such
evangelical churches have been subjected to the same denial
of their right to exist. And the matter becomes more difficult as *county* planning commissions are created, so that both
city and county now govern the right of existence for the
church. This denial, through the subterfuge of zoning laws,
of the right to exist to certain churches, has been upheld by
the U. S. Supreme Court, a fact which should surprise no
one.[15] The courts, meanwhile, are extending the ancient freedom of Christianity to irreligion, so that it is no longer necessary to believe in God to qualify as an objector to military
service.[16]

In some cities and counties, as the subdivider of a new
housing development plans his tract with the planning commission, provision is made for three religious bodies only, a
Roman Catholic Church, a synagogue, and a Protestant church
which is on the approved list. These local plans, be it noted,
reflect the ideas of national bodies, both urban planning and
religious organizations. An unapproved church is barred
from the development. In the name of "civil rights," some
lots or homes may sometimes be sold to Negroes, and the
courts increasingly further such action, which conforms to

---

[14] Glenwood Blackmore, "It Can Happen Here!," *Religious Digest*,
May, 1947, vol. 20, no. 140, p. 21; from *United Evangelical Action*,
March 15, 1947.

[15] See Ralph I. Yarnell, "Why Your Church Can't Be Built," in
American Mercury, November, 1959, vol. LXXXIX, no. 430, pp. 136-138.

[16] See "Court Says No 'God' Needed in 'Religion,'" in *The Presbyterian Journal*, February 5, 1964, vol. XXII, no. 41, p. 4.

the religon of humanity, but a church can be denied the right
of purchase in the name of planning.

Another aspect of this struggle is the outright elimination
of churches and sometimes private schools as well from a city
by zoning. This can be done in two ways. The first is by a
quota system. An editorial in a California paper cites this
method:

> It is interesting to note that the Los Altos Hills Town
> Council has once again emphasized the fact that it is op-
> posed to churches.
>
> The present plan of the city calls for not more than
> eight per cent of total land area to be used for other than
> residential use. Since churches fall into that category
> and location of Foothill College in the area more than
> over subscribes the allotted non-residential use, land for
> church use is taboo unless additional annexations are pro-
> posed.
>
> Religious liberties and civil liberties go hand in hand.
> Here is a golden opportunity for some one to fight for a
> worthy cause. Is anybody willing?[17]

This quota system can prevent new churches from coming in,
as in Los Altos Hills, or eliminate all churches from the beginning, in totally new communities. Exception to the quota
system is made where public schools are concerned, of course!

The second means is to leave out churches directly,
eliminating them from every kind of zone, business, industrial,
or residential. All kinds of reasons are mobilized to show
how undesirable the church is in any and all these zones.

The arrogance, moreover, of the enemies of religious
liberty is staggering. In one small, rural town of less than
4,000 population, famous in the state as a church town, a
new school teacher objected bitterly to the Lutheran Church

---

[17] *Los Altos News*, Thursday, November 7, 1963, p. 18. It should
be noted that Los Altos and Los Altos Hills are two different cities.
For more on the Los Altos Hills situation, see the *Los Altos News*,
Thursday, December 20, 1962, p. 2; Thursday, January 3, 1963, p. 1;
Thursday, January 10, 1963, pp. 1, 14; see also a letter from Clyde
Bedell, p. 2. Thursday, January 31, 1963, which reads in part: "Los
Altos Hills now has a synagogue, new and on ample acreage. A Catholic
church has been allowed for, on ample acreage. But NO MORE. Our
planning commission says further churches would reduce our taxable
land area. Is this Russia, or a Freudian Socialist state? Since when is
the church dispensable in the normal American community?"

bell, a delight to the community and with a history of about
80 or more years in two churches behind it. The bell rang at
9:30 each Sunday morning, and the teacher complained that
it awakened him and infringed upon his liberty!

Another means of eliminating certain *types* of churches
is by denying permission to new church bodies to begin their
existence modestly in homes. A California newspaper report
cities an instance of such regulations under the title, "Use
of homes as churches to be curbed."

> Redwood City. The use of homes as "part time"
> churches will be strongly discouraged under new policy
> amendments approved Wednesday by the San Mateo
> County Planning Commission.
> Architectural designs of proposed churches, along
> with site plans, will be required prior to approval of
> church use permits in residential areas.
> If the same space is proposed for use both for living
> and religious services, planners will not approve the per-
> mit, according to the revised policy.
> Assistant county planning director Larz Anderson,
> who drew up the policy amendments, said this was not in-
> tended to prohibit rectories or ministers' homes from
> being located on the same property as churches.
> The amendments also specify that churches must be
> located on a minimum of 20,000 square feet of land, and
> provide for posting of a bond to control compliance with
> these conditions.[18]

The Christian Church of the New Testament era would
have been eliminated by such zoning laws, because, while it
spread extensively across the empire, numbering possibly
half a million, its numbers were mostly limited in the local
churches, and all met in homes. There is no record of any
church buildings in the New Testament.

Today, these laws are an effective deterrent to theological
revolt. Many of the small, conservative and growing churches
of today began in the thirties and forties, meeting in homes,
in protest against the liberal trends in the major churches.

---

[18] *Palo Alto Times*, Thursday, December 5, 1963, p. 8. For a similar
type of situation in another community, see Tuesday, December 3, 1963,
p. 14: "Menlo Park church loses permit because of violations"; the
church involved was the Starlight Missionary Church, apparently a
Negro group. See also, in the same newspaper, Tuesday, December 3,
1963, p. 3: "SM County church land amendments to be studied."

For a handful of five or ten persons, sometimes actually supporting a pastor, to rent facilities or purchase property is prohibitive. Continued protest is thus cut off at the roots when people cannot revolt against the churches which are a part of the Establishment without being required to have all the means of institutional maturity.

Curbing or banning the use of homes as churches is also a very serious road-block to the formation of new Negro church bodies. Historically, the church in the home has a major role here. Today, as some Negroes are unhappy over the social gospel emphasis in their established churches, and hanker for the old time religion, they are confronted with a new time law which says in effect, Thou shalt not worship God except as the state allows it.

The religious broadcasting rights of conservative groups have long been under attack. Repeatedly, attempts have been made to bar "non-cooperating" Protestant groups from radio and television, sometimes with some success. Valiant battle against these infringements of liberty have been waged by some groups, among whom the *Christian Beacon* and Carl McIntire have been notable. A similar battle is being waged against broadcasting by economic and political conservatives, and, on December 19, 1961, on the request of U.S. Attorney General Robert Kennedy, Victor Reuther submitted "The Reuther Memorandum to the Attorney General of the United States," calling for infringement of liberties for conservatives. Congressman Charles Gubser of California reported that the proposed suppression of such liberties to conservatives had been started in the Federal Communication Commission's "Fairness Doctrine."[19]

Another means of attack on the freedom of the church is through legislation aimed at furthering "tolerance." Actually, the only tolerance in such proposed legislation is for the religion of humanity. For the religion of Jesus Christ, there is only intolerance. Such proposed legislation followed quickly after the organization of the United Nations, and the late 1940's saw attempts at wholesale regimentation of religious thought. Failing this, piecemeal legislation has since then been introduced, and in some areas passed.

---

[19] Charles Gubser, "On Capitol Hill," *Los Altos (Calif.) News,* Thursday, December 5, 1963, p. 24.

Let us examine the wholesale legislation as it was proposed in California, but failed to pass. In the California Legislature, 1949 Regular Session, Assembly Bill No. 403 was introduced on January 12, 1949 by Messrs. Rosenthal, Gaffney, Crowley, Hawkins, Elliott, Lewis, Rumford and Thomas:

> An act to add Section 421 to the Penal Code, relating to the discrediting of a religious denomination or a person because of his religious belief.

> The people of the State of California do enact as follows:

> Section 1. Section 421 is added to the Penal Code, to read:

> 421. Any person who promulgates any propaganda designed to belittle, ridicule, upbraid, condemn or hold up to scorn and contempt, any religious system or denomination, or otherwise attempt to discredit any church, synagogue, temple or religious institution or denomination duly incorporated in this State; or libels or slanders any such church, synagogue, temple or religious denomination; or holds up to scorn and contempt and ridicule any person or group because of his or their religious belief or worship shall be guilty of a misdemeanor.

On January 13 of the same 1949 session, the much longer Assembly Bill No. 529 was introduced, also failing to pass, called "An Act to prohibit the advocation of hatred by reason of race, color or religion, and effectuate the Bill of Rights, and providing penalties." The first bill provided a penalty, as a misdemeanor, of six months maximum imprisonment or a fine not to exceed $500, or both. The second bill, in Section 3, set forth a maximum fine of $10,000 and imprisonment not to exceed 2 years or both, also disenfranchisement for 10 years. The second bill effectually nullified in intent the preaching of orthodox Christianity, of anything except the religion of humanity. As Paul R. Cowles of Berkeley, California, in a Newsletter of March 5, 1949, commented:

> This means that if one is faithful to the BIBLE, GOD'S WORD: and preaches in accordance therewith, *THAT ANY RELIGION OR DENOMINATION WHO OR WHICH DENIES THE NEED OF THE BLOOD ATONEMENT OF JESUS CHRIST ON CALVARY: OR DENIES THE DEITY OF CHRIST. . . . ARE SINNERS AND UNSAVED, DESTINED TO ETERN-*

AL PUNISHMENT; would be a violator of these proposed laws.[20]

Since then, the piecemeal approach has been used. "Tolerance" regulations govern state college campuses, and, in various ways, the religion of humanity is being equated with the only possible moral or legal standard.

It is apparent that, in all this, orthodox Christianity has two great open enemies, the heretical liberal clergy and churches, and the courts. It is interesting to note that liberal churchmen have been ready to defend Henry Miller's books and Communists in the name of liberty while denying the right of existence to orthodox Christianity.

Tyranny, as was noted earlier, was in its origin secularism, a rule founded on man-made laws. This secularism is the religion of humanity, the most oppressive, dangerous and persecuting of all cults, because it has no law beyond itself as a check to its lust for power. Christianity is being disestablished in the several states of the United States of America only to make way for the savage establishment of the religion of humanity. The goal of this new religion is the "kingdoms of this world," and it is ready to bless and give a part in that kingdom to the true church on one condition: "All these things will I give thee, if thou wilt fall down and worship me." The answer, however, was made long ago in the wilderness: "Then said Jesus unto him, Get thee hence, Satan: for it is written, Thou shalt worship the Lord thy God, and him only shalt thou serve" (Matthew 4:9, 10).

In the name of civil defense, it is already planned that, in the next war, the orthodox "non-cooperating" churches will be denied their status as valid churches. Unregistered clergy will have no rights to minister to the sick and the dying. Any such clergy trying to minister to their flock "will find a shotgun in his belly," according to a Civil Defense leader.[21]

---

[20] Mimeographed Newsletter, Paul R. Cowles. In a letter of April 4, 1949, an "Open Letter" to Mr. J. Munroe Warner, Executive Director, East Bay Fellowship (Catholic-Jew-Protestant), whose fellowship endorsed the bills, Cowles called the measures, if enacted, "a long, long step toward totalitarianism," p. 3.

[21] Cited by Rev. T. Robert Ingram, sermon, "The Government Plan for Seizure of the Churches," March 3, 1962, St. Thomas' Episcopal Church, Houston, Texas.

One final note: on June 25, 1962, when the U.S. Supreme Court banned a simple non-compulsory prayer from New York schools, it also issued a decision which reversed a Post Office order banning from the mails three magazines aimed at homosexuals. The vote was six to one. Justice Harlan, who gave the court's opinion, stated that "these magazines are printed primarily for homosexuals and have no literary, scientific or other merit." In spite of this admission by what one writer called "a kind of legal double-talk,"[22] the ban was lifted. Obscenity laws are being made increasingly invalid by court decisions. In the same day, in the name of liberty, prayer was banned, and the propagation of perversion permitted.

A grim parallel comes to mind. A man who is increasingly a hero of some modern liberals is the Marquis de Sade (1740-1814).[23] Sade was a follower of Marat, and, with Robespierre, a member of the Section des Piques. The Marquis de Sade approved heartily of the execution of Jesus Christ while calling for total freedom for every kind of sexual perversion. For Sade, "true wisdom" meant, "not . . . . repressing our vices . . . since these vices constitute almost the only happiness in our life" and "to repress them would be to become our own executioners," but rather true wisdom "consists in abandoning ourselves to them with such secrecy, and such extensive precautions that we may never be caught out. Do not be afraid that this may diminish their delight: mystery adds to the pleasure."[24]

The Marquis de Sade wrote on religion in his *La Philosophie dans le Boudoir,* stating:

> We need a faith, a faith suited to the republican character and far removed from ever possibly resuming that of Rome. In an age when we are so convinced that religion must rest upon morality, and not morality upon religion, we need a religion in tune with our way of life, as it were the development, the inevitable extension of it, a religion which can elevate the soul and keep it

---

[22] Dr. Louis Berg M. D. in Foreword p. 8 to Michael Leigh: *The Velvet Underground.* New York: Macfadden, 1963.

[23] For evidence of this, see the introduction of Leonard de Saint-Yves to *Selected Writings of De Sade,* New York: British Book Centre, 1954. For an appreciation of Sade in an ostensibly conservative journal, see Mary Graham Lund, "The Century of De Sade," *Modern Age,* Winter 1963-64, vol. 8, no. 1, pp. 38-44.

[24] DeSade, p. 215f.

perpetually at the level of that precious liberty which it venerates today as its only idol.[25]

These ideas were, as he indicated, common to the revolutionary thought of his day, and subsequently as well. Sade, however, was prepared to apply his rationalism more systematically.

The Marquis called for the abolition "for ever (of) the atrocity of the death penalty," one of his reasons being, "it has never stamped out crime." Laws against theft he saw as inconsistent with "the maintenance of perfect equality between citizens, the equal submission of all to the law protecting the property of all." A law is not very just if it "orders the man with nothing to respect the man with everything."[26] Sade also opposed laws against prostitution, adultery, incest, rape and sodomy. Immorality and immodesty are necessary, he felt, for true republicanism. Moreover, marriage and monogamy are wrong.

> An act of possession can never be exercised over a free being. The exclusive possession of a woman is as unjust as the ownership of slaves; all men are born free, all are equal in their rights. Never forget these principles. According to them, therefore, no one sex can ever be granted a legitimate right to take exclusive possession of the other, and one of these sexes or one of these classes can never possess the other arbitrarily.[27]

For Sade, orthodox Christian theology and morality were false and should be illicit, banned by law. True equality made them impossible to accept.

For Sade, whatever can occur in Nature is morally permissible, hence homosexuality (sodomy) was natural and good. "Can we possibly imagine Nature giving us the possibility of committing a crime which would offend her?"[28] Murder too he saw as virtue. "The most independent of men and those closest to Nature are savages; with impunity they devote themselves to murder every day."[29]

To cite more is unnecessary. Sade's religion of humanity only ended up in total inhumanity, and with the confinement

---

[25] *Ibid.*, p. 237.
[26] *Ibid.*, pp. 248-253.
[27] *Ibid.*, p. 256.
[28] *Ibid.*, 258.
[29] *Ibid.*, p. 266.

of Sade as criminally insane. The religion of humanity, by subordinating the moral order to man rather than to God, enthrones anarchy and chaos. It begins with idealism and ends in the dark saturnalia of equality in death.

CHAPTER V

NEUTRALISM

One of the persistent errors of the modern era, clearly apparent in Descartes and enthroned by the Enlightenment, is the concept of neutralism. Not without deep roots in Greek and scholastic thought, it came into its own when philosophy began, with Descartes, to know man and the universe in terms of man. It was assumed that man can identify himself in terms of himself and that man and man's autonomous mind is the ultimate standard of life. The point of reference is man, and man's knowledge is independent knowledge. Man's knowledge is tested by man himself, who is thus the final court of appeal.

Although this is a highly theoretical question, it is one of intensely practical import. What are its implications?

At the time of the American Revolution, the population of the United States, approximately three million, included only 20,000 Roman Catholics at most, including their slaves, and at most 3,000 Jews. The white Protestant population was predominantly English, Scotch, and Scotch-Irish, with some Germans, Swedes, French, and Hollanders. The main religious division was between Calvinists and Arminians. There were a limited number of Deists also. The Quakers were strong in Pennsylvania but limited elsewhere, and, by their opposition to the war, declined in strength and influence. There was, on the whole, a remarkable homogeneity in the thirteen colonies and the young Union, but the divisions of opinion were very real and also serious. The influx of Jacobin opinion and subversion made that quickly apparent.

In the United States, in the latter half of the 20th century, Jews and Roman Catholics are fairly strong, and the forces of irreligion are also very extensive. Politicians speak of a Protestant vote, a Jewish vote, and a Catholic vote, as well as of Negro, labor, Southern, pensioner, farm, white-collar and other voting blocs. In many major cities, as well as some states, a ballot ticket, to win, requires candidates drawn from particular groups, i.e., Catholic, Jewish, labor, Polish, Irish, Italian, or the like. The politicians are fully aware of the fact that there is no neutrality in voting and that no vote is a neutrality vote.

In spite of this fact, it is regarded as an unforgivable political sin ever to admit this patent and open lack of neutrality. Any man who refers to the obvious fact that each and every one of these groups has deep personal commitments, beliefs and hostilities, is guilty of a most dastardly sin, except perhaps if he accuses the Protestant majority of prejudice. All are without exception "good Americans." All are interested, without exception, in the common welfare.

As a result, we have *the major hypocrisy* of American life, the *assumption* for all public purposes that all Americans share a common dedication to the general welfare, irrespective of race, color or creed, together with the *practice* of political plunder by every group capable of commiting it. With rank hypocrisy, politicians cater to race, color, creed, class, locality, and to age groups as well as to professional groups, while refusing to admit that this is a major fact and problem of American life. We have therefore an ugly fact tearing at the very entrails of the Union going hand in hand with the hypocritical insistence that the situation does not exist!

So deeply is the myth of neutralism imbedded, that to deal realistically and honestly with it is tantamount to political suicide. Politicians must assure every last plundering faction of its sanctimonious neutralism while also insisting on their own. Each particular faction, of course, insists on its own impartial, neutral and objective stance while deploring the partisan and subjective position of its adversaries. All are equally committed to the great modern myth that such a neutrality is possible. This myth is basic to classical liberalism and to most schools of thought, conservative and radical, which are derived from it.

The hypocrisy of neutralism goes deeper than politics, moreover. In one educational institution, to cite a specific instance, the president, most insistent on the scientific objectivity of scholarship, was equally anxious to add a Jew to his administrative staff. When none of the known qualified Jews proved to be either interested or available on the offered terms, it was suggested by another minority representative that the idea of a Jew as a Jew per se was an objectionable standard and that any qualified person be chosen. The comment was rejected by the president as evidence of veiled and deep-rooted prejudice! Far more serious examples of the absurdity and extent of the hypocrisy of neutralism can be cited, but our concern is not with cases but with the basic concept which makes this fantastic and schizophrenic hypocrisy possible.

In part, a liberal myth is involved, namely, that the only true loyalty is a *world* loyalty, so that any "limited" loyalty is dishonorable and should not be ascribed to honorable men. A true statesman is a man of "world vision," who sees things in terms of world politics rather than "limited" national concerns. Some would regard it as a catastrophe for an American president to be governed by American principles and interests. Perhaps an indication of this was a news comment of late 1963:

> British officials are reported to have regarded the new U.S. President, at first, as an "unmitigated disaster," because of the stress he placed on being an American. After talks with President Johnson, the British felt reassured.[1]

Others are insistent on seeing a common faith in different heritages. Thus, it is insisted that Roman Catholics and Protestants are essentially agreed, except for minor differences, although every earnest Catholic and Protestant knows that the differences are not minor but basic and vital. Judaism is also brought into the same generous tent, and reference is made to "our Judeo-Christian heritage," again an offense to earnest believers. To the truly religious Jew, Christianity is a diversion and a perversion of the true faith and is at best unrealistically weak where it appears most promising for man. For the Christian, Phariseeism, Saduceeism, and Essenism were departures from biblical faith, and all the nation was in heresy and apostasy when it crucified Christ. Since then, through Talmudic developments, the theological

---

[1] "Washington Whispers," *U. S. News & World Report,* December 16, 1963, vol. LV, no. 25, p. 22.

rift has widened, not diminished.[2]   The term "Judeo-Christian" is most commonly used by the adherents of the religion
of humanity, who are insistent on reading their religion into
both Judaism and Christianity. No doubt, if Buddhism were
a factor on the American scene, we would hear references
to our Buddho-Judeo-Christian heritage.

More basic to this problem than this unlimited world
loyalty myth is the myth of man's neutralism. It is assumed
that all men are interested in the general welfare, and, if
they are not, they are guilty of some fearful depravity.

This, unhappily, is the perspective of both liberals and
conservatives. For the liberal, the conservative stands self-
condemned because he so clearly reveals a limited loyalty and
an obvious lack of neutrality. He is patently a nationalist,
or an isolationist, or perhaps a States rights man (or even
a county rights man), and is hostile to the United Nations,
to the U.S.S.R., to foreign aid, and to other shibboleths of
neutralism. Before such depravity, they stand aghast, and,
like a high priest of old, rend their garments at this blasphemy, declaring, "what further need have we of witnesses?
behold, now ye have heard his blasphemy" (Matt. 26:65).
Without question, this horror is usually genuine, and it is
touching. It is evidence of a religious faith because it is so
clearly a religious horror.

And the conservatives, who are so often the objects of
this holy dismay, themselves reveal it as they deal with others.
A specific instance can be cited. Much use, with appropriate
horror, has been made of an American Jewish Committee
publication, *Committee Reporter,* because of an article en-
titled "Christmas in July," calling for a campaign against
Christmas religious observances in statist schools. The information was reported in the Catholic weekly, the *Brooklyn
Tablet,* January 21, 1956, and widely reprinted or cited. To
this news the conservatives have reacted with horror, with
rending of garments, and with shock at this great blasphemy.

The question needs to be faced bluntly: How else should
a loyal Jew behave? Should he promote that which is hostile
to his faith? "Subversion," yes, but what are Christian
missionaries doing in Israel, or in Japan, but trying to "sub-

---

[2] In 1870, Auerbach acknowledged openly the long tacit assumption
that the Talmud is "the law of God." Feliks Koneczny: *On the Plurality of Civilisations,* p. 257, London: Polonica, 1962.

vert" the existing religious order? And was it not a part of official U.S. policy to "disestablish" and discredit Shintoism in conquered Japan? And did not General Douglas MacArthur issue a call from occupied Japan for Christian missionaries?

Jews in Israel are as horrified at Christian activities and hopes in their country, as Christians in America are at Jewish efforts. And Christians in Israel see it as an instance of tyranny or evil if such horror is expressed, while Jews in America are equally shocked if their efforts are resisted. All are so ridiculously convinced of their impartiality, nobility, and neutrality, that to ascribe a limited and partisan perspective to them is to charge them with a fearful moral shame.

But men are never more foolish nor more dangerous than when they delude themselves into believing that they act for the general welfare. It is then that they begin to play at being gods, assuming a lofty and god-like title of superiority to and transcendence of the normal human greeds and lusts. Men are never more susceptible to the sins which so easily beset humanity as when they believe themselves to be beyond them or immune to them. It is then that the good of mankind becomes readily equated with the fulfilment of man's sin, and blinded by their delusions, men grope for the wall in the noonday sun.

Conservatives would not be prone to this delusion of neutralism if they were consistently and theologically Christian. One of the privileges of being a Christian is that a Christian can accept the fact that he is a creature, and, moreover, a sinful creature, and that he stands before God, not in his righteousness but in the righteousness of Jesus Christ.

Neutralism is a myth. Man cannot transcend himself to view the human situation with a godlike objectivity. He will always view things from his perspective, as a Protestant, Catholic, Jew, Buddhist or the like, as a farmer, laborer, professional man or an educator. He can approach others with charity and with justice, assuring them of their God-given rights to life, home, property, and immunity from false witness, even as he expects to receive these immunities himself. He must always be aware of his limitations as a creature and find in it his liberty, for to seek a liberty beyond our capacities is to ask for slavery.

The constitutional convention did not expect Americans to act in terms of the common welfare. Instead, they were aware of the lack of neutrality and were concerned with nullifying its effects by various structural and legal checks and balances.

In *The Federalist,* this problem was discussed by James Madison in the 10th paper. The reality of factions was assumed: the problem was their control. "Among the numerous advantages promised by a well-constructed Union, none deserves to be more accurately developed than its tendency to break and control the violence of faction." Madison then defined a faction, and, to his credit, made it clear that a faction, among other things could be "a majority or minority of the whole." No group can claim to transcend factionalism, therefore, simply because it commands an overwhelming following:

> By a faction, I understand a number of citizens, whether amounting to a majority or minority of the whole, who are united and actuated by some common impulse of passion, or of interest, adverse to the rights of other citizens, or to the permanent and aggregate interests of the community.

There are "two methods of curing the mischiefs of faction: the one, by removing its causes; the other, by controlling its effects." There are, similarly, "two methods of removing the causes of faction: the one, by destroying the liberty which is essential to its existence; the other, by giving to every citizen the same opinions, the same passions and the same interests." For Madison, the first remedy is "worse than the disease," because it posits the destruction of liberty, which, while nourishing faction, also nourished the basic health of political life. "The second expedient is as impracticable as the first would be unwise." Madison then made a very significant comment:

> As long as the reason of man continues fallible, and he is at liberty to exercise it, different opinions will be formed. As long as the connection subsists between his reason and his self-love, his opinions and his passions will have a reciprocal influence on each other; and the former will be objects to which the latter will attach themselves. The diversity in the faculties of men, from which the rights of property originate, is not less an

insuperable obstacle to a uniformity of interests. The protection of these faculties is the first object of government. From the protection of different and unequal faculties of acquiring property, the possession of different degrees and kinds of property immediately results; and from the influence of these on the sentiments and views of the respective proprietors, ensues a division of the society into different interests and parties.

The latent causes of faction are thus sown in the nature of man; and we see them everywhere brought into different degrees of activity, according to the different circumstances of civil society.

First of all, Madison denied the doctrine of neutralism. He denied the Enlightenment faith in the objectivity of reason, which, in Christian terms, he saw as inalienably tied to self-love. Man's reasoning is thus not objective reasoning; it is personal reasoning and will be thus governed by "the nature of man" rather than an abstract concept of rationality. Second, while avoiding all invidious comparisons between men, Madison pointed out that men have differing abilities. These diverse abilities or "faculties" lead to diverse stations and to differing desires and capabilities with respect to the acquisition of property. Some would be great landowners and farmers; others would have an urban concept of property, others a monetary one. Some would be, on the other hand, drifters. Some would be wealthy, others would be of the middle class, and some would be laborers. *The Federalist* and the Constitution presuppose this diversity as natural. Third, "The protection of these faculties is the first object of government." True government and true liberty, in other words, require the protection of human differences, and, implicitly, of those things productive of factions. To equalize men is thus to deny the very function of civil government. Civil government should provide that just order which is necessary for the development of the differing abilities of men, not to attempt their equalization or to compel a forced fraternization.

It would follow, therefore, that a "bi-partisan foreign policy" is a denial of liberty, in that it asserts that there can be only one acceptable theory of foreign relations in the body politic. Not surprisingly, it goes hand in hand with an intolerance of every opinion in either party except the so-called "dynamic center."

Madison felt that religious differences, among other things, would be productive of factions, although, historically, property has been "the most common and durable source of factions" because of "unequal distribution." He did not therefore propose the abolition of either but was, of course, the champion of the liberty of both. What was obvious to Madison was "that the *causes* of faction cannot be removed, and that relief is only to be sought in the means of controlling its effects." Democracies by seeking to remove the *causes,* only *aggravated* the conflict and destroyed liberty:

> From this view of the subject it may be concluded that a pure democracy, by which I mean a society consisting of a small number of citizens, who assemble and administer the government in person, can admit of no cure for the mischief of faction. A common passion or interest will, in almost every case, be felt by a majority of the whole; a communication and concert result from the form of government itself; and there is nothing to check the inducements to sacrifice the weaker party or an obnoxious individual. Hence it is that such democracies have ever been spectacles of turbulence and contention; have ever been found incompatible with personal security or the rights of property; and have in general been as short in their lives as they have been violent in their deaths. Theoretic politicians, who have patronized this species of government, have erroneously supposed that by reducing mankind to a perfect equality in their political rights, they would, at the same time, be perfectly equalized and assimilated in their possessions, their opinions, and their passions.

Any attempt therefore to remove faction and attain to a pure democracy is foredoomed, since faction springs from the very nature of man and of his diverse faculties. To assume that the differences of ability, race, color and creed are not productive of faction is a folly of "theoretic politicians," and, we might add, of mendacious ones.

The answer, for Madison, is in a republic, more specifically, in the federal union of the Constitution, which, with its various checks and balances, its varieties of civil structure, is "a republican remedy for the diseases more incident to republican government."[3]

---

[3] The Edward Mead Earle edition of *The Federalist,* pp. 53-62, New York: Modern Library, 1937, has been here used.

It is precisely this historic, constitutional answer which is today being denied by president, Congress, courts, and by many people. The demand is for democracy, and for the suppression of those differences which Madison said that civil government existed to protect. It is now an insult to assume that a Protestant is a Protestant, a Roman Catholic a Roman Catholic, a Jew a Jew, a Negro a Negro, or that a farmer, laborer, banker, or any other person is what he is. A common neutralism must be ascribed to all as the only honorable approach.

Ironically, these same persons will be often strict environmentalists, or geneticists, in their approach to criminality and to "mental health." In these areas, man has no responsibility. He is a product of past forces and present pressures. But, in this schizophrenic perspective, man, transferred to the political arena, is suddenly endowed with a godlike objectivity and neutrality. He transcends himself and his situation.

The orthodox Christian cannot deny responsibility for sin without denying the biblical doctrine of man. But man's responsibility and his ability is that of a creature, so that he is always and without exception before God in an historical, personal and an involved situation. This is not a denial of liberty but an affirmation that, because man is a creature, his is the limited liberty of a creature rather than the absolute liberty of an absolute God.

Thus, the concept of *the bland American*, neutral and objective, is a myth and a dangerous myth. Faction must be recognized as a reality, and factions must be identified as factions, the white Protestant majority no less than the Jewish minority. And it must be accepted that each will reflect his perspective. But what must be required of all is the common structure and restraint of law.

The biblical law of love for neighbor and enemy is cited in Scripture repeatedly (Lev. 19, Matt. 19, Rom. 13) as a summation of the second table of the law. As Frederick Nymeyer has shown, in *Progressive Calvinism* and *First Principles*, the second table of the law is the basic charter of man's God-given liberties and rights, to life ("thou shalt not kill"), to the sanctity of his home ("thou shalt not commit adultery"), for his property ("thou shalt not steal"), for the integrity of his reputation ("thou shalt not bear false witness"), and for their protection from intent as well as deed ("thou shalt not covet").

The factional American therefore must live under God and under law because he is not capable himself of a god-like neutrality. The concept of *the bland American* is thus an anti-Christian ideal and a denial of not only the reality which the Constitution recognized but of that order which God created.

The bland scholar and *the bland university,* is similarly a myth, as is the apparent United Nations ideal of *the bland man.* No person or institution possesses the ability to be neutral and objective, to transcend itself and its historical context. This is no less true of science. Some would claim for the instruments of science, if not for scientists, this capacity for neutrality. But do scientific instruments make for *objectivity?* They are *the refinement of a perspective,* namely, that the *truth or utility* of a thing rests *in measurement,* a highly debatable proposition. Scientific instruments are helpful, towards *accuracy* for a perspective, but they do not thereby give it *truth, objectivity* or *neutrality.*

As Van Til has said, "In the last analysis we shall have to choose between two theories of knowledge. According to the one theory God is the final court of appeal; according to the other theory man is the final court of appeal."[4] If man is the final court of appeal, then there is no appeal beyond man, and the tyranny of man to man quickly prevails. The faction in power can assume that it is the true dictatorship of the proletariat, or the voice of the people, or the voice of humanity, and deny liberty to all other factions. Not only that, but the ruling faction can pronounce judgment on other factions and condemn them in any way it so wills. It is an inescapable fact that, if final and absolute judgment be denied to God, it will be exercised by men to the death of all liberty and social order. Damnation is not escaped by being "withdrawn" from God; it is simply transferred to man and made the instrument of total tyranny. This is the implication of ascribing neutrality to man. It is an ascription of transcendence and of divinity, and its consequences are tyranny and hell on earth.

---

[4] Cornelius Van Til: *The Defense of the Faith,* p. 51. Philadelphia: Presbyterian and Reformed, 1955.

A civil order which rests on the assumption that factions are real, and that they are "sown in the nature of man" by "the diversity in the faculties of men" which it "is the first object of government" to protect, is a civil order which assumes as a first premise the sovereign and transcendental nature of God as the only objective source of judgment, the only ultimate ground of fraternity, and the only objective mind which exists. It will therefore be a civil order which will ascribe to itself only limited functions, claiming added powers only as in pride and self-exaltation it seeks to be as god. And this it can do only if its citizens are themselves deluded into believing that they and their institutions can transcend faction and become neutral and objective powers.

The alternative to "In God we trust" is "In man we trust," or in reason, science, the experimental method, an elite, or some like entity. In any and every case, it is a *religious* affirmation. The presuppositions of all man's thinking are inescapably religious, and they are never neutral.

CHAPTER VI

THE RELIGION OF HUMANITY

The Civil War was a triumph for the religion of humanity. Most churches, whatever their stand on slavery, opposed abolitionism and its social radicalism. As a result, in the North, these churches supported the war effort rather than demanding it. The Unitarian, Universalist, and transcendentalist champions of abolition were thus the real victors of the war. They called for war, tried to promote it by financing John Brown, and, when war began, called at once for emancipation as the war aim. These men were moved, as a Unitarian scholar has pointed out, by "the perfectionist desire to impose upon the West and South the intellectual and religious supremacy of New England. One significant result of the Civil War was to accomplish just this."[1]

For this, they were in part grateful to the South for forcing the issue. Nothing served their purposes better.[2] Lincoln was a minority president who did not control Congress. The abolitionists wanted war and were afraid it would be avoided. War, after all, is a basic ingredient for revolutionary action. When the war ended, their triumph was clear-cut. The South was broken, slavery abolished, President

---

[1] Phillips: *Puritan and Unitarian Views of Church and Society in America*, p. L 1.

[2] The South was made the butt of moralistic horror. In a school book of the day, a little girl asked, "Wicked people make war, don't they?" This "truth" from a child "changed" her pro-Southern father's heart, who then spoke of "my conversion." Vina Clifford, "Dialogue: A Secessionist Saved," *The Student and Schoolmate, and Forrester's Boys and Girls Magazine*, pp. 184-6. Boston: Joseph H. Allen, 1863. The responsible leaders in the South, including Jefferson Davis, had been unfavorable to the move towards secession.

Johnson nullified in his plan for reconstruction, and, with the combination of having been laggards with respect to war and emancipation, and being assaulted as well after 1859 by Darwinism, the orthodox churches were badly hurt. They had previously dominated the intellectual scene; their opponents were rebels against it. Now they were themselves increasingly dominated by the new intellectual currents. Before 1860, most Americans felt that, however slavery was dealt with, it should not be by revolutionary action. After 1864, the voices of moderation and gradualism were tainted with the onus of having defended a now discredited system.

A representative thinker of the religion of humanity in that era was Moncure Daniel Conway (1832-1907). Conway was born in Virginia and began as a Methodist minister but soon became a Unitarian. Unitarianism itself provided for him the opportunity for "broader" horizons. He became a dedicated anti-slavery man, and then went on to head for many years the South Place Institute (for advanced religious thought) in London. For Conway, the essence of true religion is the happiness of man.

> Unhappiness is the root of all evil. From it springs meanness, vice, crime, bitterness, injustice. Happiness is the sacred spirit, the mother of virtues. What imaginable function has religion except to promote human happiness? If there be a universal Heart it suffers from every human sigh and tear, it bleeds with every falling sparrow, it "answereth man in the joy of his heart."[3]

Is it any wonder then that a generation infected by this concept of evil sees crime and delinquency merely as a need and a lack? Supply love, make happiness possible with material blessings, and goodness and all virtues must inevitably flow, according to this faith. Any inequality is to the detriment of both rich and poor, since true happiness is social and shared. Happiness, moreover, is regarded as an essential goal of the state in this philosophy. No less a person than U. S. Chief Justice Earl Warren, in his 1962 Charter Day address at the University of California, declared of the State of California, "We will have the problem of providing for the happiness of more people than any state in the Union." Instead of celebrating their numerical primacy in the Union,

---

[3] Moncure Daniel Conway: *My Pilgrimage to the Wise Men of the East.* p. 13 London: Constable: Boston: Houghton, Mifflin, 1906.

Warren urged Californians, "I would make it a day for contemplation as to how we might better provide for the happiness of these millions."[4]   This is a logical goal for the state if evil is a product, not of sin, not of immorality, but of unhappiness.   If "unhappiness is the root of all evil," as Conway held, and Warren's position implies, then social justice means that men's desires must be met.   Envy then must be satisfied, and man's every hunger met, in order to ensure "justice."   Men and society must be equalized and barriers destroyed, for "Thou shalt not" is an impediment to this concept of happiness.

Believing the religion of humanity to be the true religion behind all historical religions, Conway made a pilgrimage to the East to see these ancient wonders first hand.   He reported with pleasure on Kwan-yin, the Chinese goddess of mercy: "She is the woman who refused to enter paradise so long as any human being is excluded.   'Never will I receive individual salvation,' she said, and still remains outside the gates of heaven."[5]   On arriving in Ceylon he stated, "I had studied the Sinhalese Buddha and Buddhists, and knew I was leaving behind Anglo-Saxonism,—cruel, ambitious, canting, aggressive,—to mingle with people who knew 'the blessedness of being little'."[6]   Conway found repeated occasions to compare Christianity and the West unfavorably with the East.   Moreover, "The idea of salvation by one's own merit prevails in every religion on the face of the earth except Christianity."[7]

Conway, then, believed in a works doctrine of salvation, and for him the essence of true works was social revolution. Accordingly, he wrote, during the Civil War: "Let us consider gravely *what it is* we are carrying South as we march on.   One thing we must carry,—devastation."   This smiting of the South was for its healing, for, as the proverb says, "Faithful are the wounds of a friend."[8]   Conway spoke and wrote as "a friend" of the South. His father was a Virginian, whose body-servant, James Parker, "actually fled from free-

---

[4] Cited by George N. Crocker, "Serving Happiness on a Platter," *S. F. Examiner*, Sect. II, p. 2, Sunday, January 27, 1963.

[5] Conway: *My Pilgrimage.* p. 71.

[6] *Ibid.*, p. 108f.

[7] *Ibid.*, p. 126.

[8] Conway: *The Golden Hour*, p. 85f. Boston: Ticknor and Fields, 1862.

dom with the Northern troops to the Confederate lines," leaving behind his family in Washington, in order to be with the senior Conway.[9] The miracle of John 5:1-15 provided Conway with an analogy: the war was comparable to the pool, whose waters "Agitation, the angel of Freedom, has troubled," and in which "the diseased nation shall bathe, and be made every whit whole."[10]

Conway could not agree with Lincoln on the war aim being the preservation of the Union: "there is no Union to be preserved" as long as slavery existed to divide it. "In fact as far as the *old* Union is concerned, the only arms now defending it are in the South."[11]

"The native glow of the human heart is for justice."[12] To seek the preservation of the Union above justice was to mask a monster. Social justice required that we pronounce a "Never more!" over the old Union. Otherwise, the United States would be like Pilate, "surrendering humanity" to death. "The damned spot is in every palm: there is not water enough in all the rivers and lakes of America to wash it out."[13] Justice and brotherhood, not the Constitution, must prevail. The "rejected stone" in America was not Christ but *justice.* "The form in which it stands for us is THE AFRICAN SLAVE."[14] The slave was America's crucified Christ, whose redemption was America's redemption, and whose presence was a test and standard, "the touchstone of every virtue."[15]

In its every campaign, the religion of humanity has presented its current cause as the ultimate standard, the acid test and "touchstone of every virtue." The current cause is its Bible and creed, the party line, from which none must depart. Thus, when Charles A. Beard published his *President Roosevelt and the Coming of the War, 1941,* in 1948, he was attacked as now senile and incompetent. When, in 1963, Albert Schweitzer criticized the United Nations policy in the

---

[9] Conway, *My Pilgrimage,* p. 37.

[10] Conway: *Golden Hour,* p. 160.

[11] M. D. Conway: *The Rejected Stone; or, Insurrection vs. Resurrection in America,* by a Native of Virginia, pp. 6-8. Boston: Walker, Wise, 1962, third edition.

[12] *Ibid.,* p. 8.

[13] *Ibid.,* p.13f.

[14] *Ibid.,* p. 24.

[15] *Ibid.,* p. 26.

Congo, this liberal hero was also sadly cited as now behind the times, and as grown timid and conservative with age. There is good reason for this perspective. The religion of humanity looks to the perfection of man in paradise on earth. Not a single false stone can be laid, nor a false step taken. The future depends, not on God, but entirely on man. "For to do justice to the Negro is to lay the corner-stone of the Republic of Man. It is nothing less."[16] If need be, it follows, man must be disloyal to the present order in the name of loyalty to the future order. Any loyalty to the future means revolution, for "revolutions go not backward."[17] The founding fathers and their successors while having the door of amendment open, where "new revelations might enter," had not moved ahead. Indeed, "our nation declared for nullification of the laws of God. It declared for injustice."[18]

For Conway, the issue was "a rebellion vs. a revolution." The South was in rebellion; the North was conducting, he hoped, a revolution. If not a revolution, then the North was "actually in the same relation to the South that George the Third so lately held toward itself!" The South claimed that this was exactly the parallel.

> On the surface, and for the moment, the South is right in this. So long as the position of our Government is purely political,—so long as it remains, as now, a question of government against government, of authority against authority,—we are their obstinate George the Third; and *on that count* we are already partially, and in the end shall be completely, nonsuited.[19]

The South had charged that the issues in 1860 were the same as in 1776, namely, the attempt of a central power to overthrow the authority of the states and their self-government, that the federal union had been claiming powers which properly belonged only to the states. Northern Democrats made similar charges, noting the parallel to 1776.[20] Indeed, they

---

[16] *Ibid.*, p. 28.
[17] *Ibid.*, p. 37.
[18] *Ibid.*, p. 44.
[19] *Ibid.*, p. 76.
[20] *The Old Guard*, vol. III, no. x, October, 1865, pp. 468-470, "Titles of Rare Old English Pamphlets on the American Revolution, Compared with Modern Northern pamphlets in Relation to the South."

charged that a conspiracy was seeking to dissolve the historic federal union and to create a unitary state.[21]

For Conway, all this was justifiable *only* if the Revolution proceeded. Liberty could not be denied. "The Southern movement is, then, not a revolution, but a rebellion against the noblest of revolutions. It is a league of confederates against the peaceful and legal evolution of Liberty on this continent. It is an Insurrection against a Resurrection."[22] The revolutionary prospectus has attracted the attention of revolutionists elsewhere, Conway reported, with Garibaldi sending word to America, "If this war is for Freedom, I come with twenty thousand men."[23] The war had to be made "a war for Humanity," and "no war of Manhood was ever yet lost." "The Rejected Stone" is "JUSTICE TO MAN," and America must lay it "as the Head of the Corner in the future fabric,—the Republic of man."[24] The Negro therefore assumed a messianic role for the Civil War radicals, and William Darrah Kelley, a member of Congress for Philadelphia, said, "Yes, sneer at or doubt it as you may, the negro is the 'coming man' for whom we have waited."[25] We need not be surprised, then, that one of these champions of the religion of humanity, speaking of his fellow radicals and himself, said,

> The army of the North was to them the church militant; the leader of the army was the avenging Lord; and the reconstruction of a new order, on the basis of freedom for mankind, was the first installment of the Messianic Kingdom.[26]

Another prominent Unitarian and suffragette, Julia Ward Howe, set this faith down in song, to the tune of "John Brown's Body," "The Battle Hymn of the Republic" (1861), which begins, "Mine eyes have seen the glory of the coming of the Lord." The Union armies represented the Lord, and "The Confederacy is a serpent, which God's Hero must slay,

---

[21] The Old Guard, vol. III no. II February, 1865, pp. 91f., "Conspiracy in Congress." See also vol. I, no. 5, May, 1863, pp. 125-127, "Government by Conspiracy."

[22] Conway: *The Rejected Stone*, p. 80.

[23] *Ibid.*, p. 93.

[24] *Ibid.*, pp. 113, 115.

[25] *The Old Guard*, vol. I, no. IX, September 1863, p. 240.

[26] Octavius Brooks Frothingham: *The Religion of Humanity*, p. 20. New York: G. P. Putnam's Sons, 1875. Third Edition.

and in proportion to the punishment inflicted by this Hero on God's enemies, who are also his own, the Deity will reward the Hero."[27]

During the Civil War, a Protestant thinker commented on the extent to which the United States had been subjected to anti-Christian pressures. These forces had been especially strong because of the *political* ties with France in the early years of the country's independence, but, all things considered, "it becomes a matter of surprise that French infidelity did not acquire greater influence over our people." Now, however, a special effort was again under way, as during the first twenty-five years of national existence, to undermine the Christian faith. This effort came from Unitarian, Universalist, pantheistic and other related groups.[28]

The Positivism of Auguste Comte, and his version of the religion of humanity, perhaps could have been added to this list. In the United States, Henry Edger (1820-1888), of whose abilities Conway wrote favorably, was the leading figure of this school.[29] Comte's development and formulation of the religion of humanity had only minor influences on the American scene, however, because of its institutional orientation.

The basic impetus was in origin Unitarian, with European influences being channeled through that movement and its associated forces. It outgrew Unitarian boundaries and saw itself as "free thought." Women's suffrage, feminism, the Negro vote as well as abolition, mesmerism, spiritualism, the peace movement, vegetarianism, socialism, repeal of usury laws, and other like movements were championed by these men, as witness Warren Chase. All this was done with a humorless zeal, a belief in man's speedy perfectibility, as well as with fervent self-righteousness. Witness the self-praise which appears in Chase's autobiography, a characteristic of such literature as late as in G. Stanley Hall's autobiography:

---

[27] Edmund Wilson: *Patriotic Gore*, p. 95. For Wilson, strangely, Calvinism, which he dislikes, is somehow to blame for all this even though it be Unitarian!

[28] John Fletcher Hurst: *History of Rationalism*, pp. 536 f., 571, 573-5. New York: Hunt and Eaton, 1865.

[29] Richmond Laurin Hawkins: *Positivism in the United States* (1853-1861), p. 124. Cambridge: Harvard University Press, 1938.

Through this correspondence (with various women) his soul's highest and holiest affections were cultivated, expanded, and ripened, like the flowers of June under the glowing sunlight. His heart grew rich in fragrance and purity, and shed its influence on others; thus rendering himself still more and more an object of suspicion, jealousy, and gossip for the wicked and corrupt, who could see no motive for any man to converse or correspond with females except a lustful or licentious one, as none other could prompt such acts in themselves. Little did they know how much he pitied their condition, and deplored their depravity. But they could not be lifted, except by long years of "prayer and fasting," from their slavish and brutal conditions.[30]

The characteristics commonly ascribed to Puritanism were best descriptive of the Unitarians. Certainly Charles Sumner was the epitome of self-righteous zeal and humorless self-importance.[31]

The movement, moreover, was characterized by an anarchy of ideas and impulses, with every man playing his own god and hostile therefore to the "popery" of Comte. O. B. Frothingham in particular objected to Comte's appropriation of the name, "The Religion of Humanity." In his book of that title, Frothingham denied that the ideas of this faith

---

[30] Warren Chase: *Life-Line of the Lone One*, p. 152. Chase hated Christianity as "idolatry" and went "beyond" Pantheism to "spiritualism." He was a leader in a socialist phalanx or colony in Wisconsin, which soon failed, and was soon thereafter very prominent in the state legislature. Chase believed that only the Oneida Colony and the Shakers practised true Christianity with respect to marriage, p. 207f. For Chase, hate was a form of sickness, p. 291, and love and forgiveness were to be unconditionally extended: "They are forgiven, for they know not what they do . . . Love hath every magic power to chase away all sin," p. iv, cf. 146. G. Stanley Hall (1846-1924) believed himself to be the equal of Jesus or Buddha, *Life and Confessions of a Psychologist*, p. 596; New York: Appleton, 1927.

[31] The caricatures of Puritans best fit the Unitarians, and Sumner is but one example among many. Sumner, as a youth, came late to breakfast one morning. When reproved by his mother, he rebuked her in return: "Call me Mr. Sumner, mother, if you please." Noah Brooks reported: "He once told me that he never allowed himself even in the privacy of his chamber, to fall into a position which he would not take in his chair in the Senate," Lloyd Paul Stryker: *Andrew Johnson, A Study in Courage*, p. 42; New York: Macmillan, 1929. Sumner was so unhappy over Longfellow's marriage that the Longfellows in pity took him on their wedding trip, whereupon Sumner read, on the train trip, Bossuet's funeral orations to the newlyweds, David Donald: *Charles*

were Comte's. "If the name was of his invention the thing is not."[32]

Octavius Brooks Frothingham (1822-1895), like so many others of this school a Harvard man, was the son of a distinguished Unitarian clergyman, Nathaniel Langdon Frothingham (1793-1870), pastor of the First Unitarian Church of Boston, 1815-1850. The father held to the older school of Unitarianism, bent upon liberalizing Christianity, upon expanding it rather than transcending it. His sermons indicate only mildly his dissent with the basic doctrines of Christianity, because, despite his belief that a true doctrine with respect to Easter owned "no dependence upon time," he still clung to the form of the Christian faith and calendar.[33] His son, after 1867, separated from 'orthodox' Unitarianism. Transcendentalism had already exerted a major influence on the younger Frothingham, and a major history of that school of thought was written by him.[34] Subsequently, he became president of the Free Religious Association and, in 1873, he questioned the propriety of the inclusion of his name in the Unitarian Year-book list of ministers, since the editor of the *Christian Register* had urged those "who have ceased to accept Jesus as pre-eminently their spiritual leader and teacher" to withdraw from Unitarianism. A long controversy ensued, and after relegation for one year to a supplementary list, all free-thought clergymen "were restored in 1884, with the ap-

_____

Sumner and the Coming of the Civil War, p. 95. Donald, who should know better, calls this Unitarian Sumner, p. 388, "the voice of puritanism in politics"! The pompous role of Sumner was cited by Carl Schurz as an admirable trait in his Eulogy: "He felt in himself the whole dignity of the Republic." *A Memorial of Charles Sumner*, p. 238, printed by Order of the Legislature, Boston, 1874. Some Unitarians, especially Transcendentalists, found the natural toilet functions a horror. The classic retort here was made by another Unitarian of sorts, Daniel Webster. When he bumped into Margaret Fuller as she was coming out of a privy, he murmered reverently, "with his beaver at his breast," to the embarrassed "emancipated" woman, "Madam, we are fearfully and wonderfully made," George Howe: *Mount Hope, A New England Chronicle*, p. 193; New York: Viking Press, 1959.

[32] O. B. Frothingham: *The Religion of Humanity*, p. 32.

[33] N. L. Frothingham: *Sermons, in the Order of a Twelvemonth*, p. 84. Boston: Crosby, Nichols, 1852.

[34] O. B. Frothingham: *Transcendentalism in New England;* New York: G. P. Putnam's Sons, 1876, reprinted with an introduction of Sydney E. Ahlstrom in 1959 as a Harper Torchbook.

proval of both Association and Conference."[35]   Free-thought was now acceptable Unitarianism.

For O. B. Frothingham, the religion of humanity meant very definitely the worship of humanity. His Christ or Savior was "the Christ of Humanity." "Humanity is the highest known form of organized existence." "The race has demanded a deity with affections," who is truly human, "who is not so much a man as Man."[36]   Moreover, "Our Christ is not so much a community as an element that is the soul of many communities." Even as Paul spoke of the church as one body, an organism, so is humanity "an individual," one body. History is the autobiography of this Christ of humanity. This Christ "satisfies our conception of an eternal being, for we can assign to him no beginning and we can prophecy (sic) for him no end. . . He is omniscient, for he possesses all the knowledge there is, He is omnipotent, for he has the resources of all power. . Unchangeable he is, save with that heavenly changeableness in which there is no mutability, but only a progress from glory to glory." Moreover, the Christ of Humanity" is sinless; for the law of his perfection is in himself, and, of course, he cannot transgress it."[37]   The import of this is obvious. Not only does Frothingham hold to a unitary and organic conception of man and society, but he also ascribes to that unitary aspect, rather than to the erring individuals, perfection and sinlessness. The state which thus embodies this religion of humanity is deified and placed beyond all criticism and law. It is by definition both the perfect order and the Christ or savior of man. The individual must therefore see all error in himself and none in the state. The sickness is in the individual if he dissents from the state, a sign of mental sickness, because the state is itself health when the state identifies itself with the religion of humanity. Salvation is thus social, in, through, and by the state. "The Christ of Humanity is the Saviour, the physician of bodies and souls. He cures our sicknesses, expels our demons, strengthens our infirmities, works miracles of healing."[38] Lest we misunderstand him, Frothingham expressed himself

[35] Earl Morse Wilbur: *A History of Unitarianism in Transylvania, England, and America*, p. 477. Cambridge: Harvard, 1952.

[36] O. B. Frothingham: *The Religion of Humanity*, p. 83 f.

[37] *Ibid.*, pp. 94-98.

[38] *Ibid.*, p. 104.

even more plainly: "Humanity, taken in its most compre-
hensive sense, is but a reflection after all of deity."[39]   Therefore, the essence of true morality is this: " 'Live for the
whole'; live so that the relation between you and others may
remain unbroken; that the currents of active sympathy may
flow evenly on; that your life may fit firmly into its frame,
and deposit its contribution just where it belongs."[40]   By
implication, to live for anything but humanity as a whole is
to be immoral, faulty or sick.

True life therefore was life in terms of humanity rather
than some supernatural God or Savior, or a nation, or any
other "limited" end.   To be separated from humanity is to
have a living death:

> Humanity has but one life, breathes but one atmos-
> phere, draws sustenance from one central orb.   To be
> reconciled with humanity, to feel the common pulse, is
> life; to be alienated from humanity, to have no share in
> the common vitality is death.   The slightest material
> separation is felt disastrously.[41]

Frothingham, while departing from orthodoxy, and from
its doctrine of the Holy Spirit and infallibility, retained these
latter concepts for his system.

> The interior spirit of any age is the spirit of God; and
> no faith can be living that has that spirit against it; no
> Church can be strong except in that alliance.   The life
> of the time appoints the creed of the time and modifies
> the establishment of the time.[42]

This indeed is the first principle of Frothingham's modernism, and it has two important aspects.   First, "The interior
spirit of any age" is made infallible and inspired.   There
can be no truth, life, or faith apart from it.   The state and
church which epitomize this "interior spirit," which is of
course identical with the religion of humanity, are infallible
and beyond criticism.   No church had ever claimed such authority unto itself as Frothingham now claimed for this new
religion and its institutions.   Second, the truth incarnated
in these forms is a changing truth: "The life of the times
appoints the creed of the time."   This is a form of relativism

---

[39] *Ibid.*, p. 106.
[40] *Ibid.*, p. 178.
[41] *Ibid.*, p. 130.
[42] *Ibid.*, p. 7f.

or pragmatism. Truth changes as "the interior spirit of the age," the religion of humanity, dictates. This doctrine is comparable to Karl Barth's conception of the "freedom" of God, i.e., His freedom to change and to be other than Himself in His laws and being.

For Frothingham, the Civil War was the order of the day. It was more than an American concern; it was "a struggle for the ultimate rights of universal man, a battle with the barbarism of the past, a life and death conflict between human nature, simple and free, and the unnatural, the preturnatural, in the European systems."[43]

However else others might view the events of the day, Frothingham saw "the soul of good in evil." This had been the case from the beginning. In the "fable" of the Garden of Eden, the serpent represents "the supreme creative purpose that comprehends centuries and a world." He tempts man "to wisdom and insight into the secret of life," to "be as gods, knowing good and evil."

> The first sin was the first triumph of virtue. The fall was the first step forward. The advent of evil was the dawn of intelligence, discernment, enterprise, aspiration. Eden was the scene of humanity's birth. The tempter was Lucifer—the bringer of light. Thus even in him is something prophetic of salvation. The fault of Adam was disobedience to spoken law; but disobedience to arbitrary spoken decree, to unreasoning command, what is that but in essence obedience to the unspoken command of intelligence, and what is that but the soul of goodness?[44]

For Frothingham, "Men are not sinners"; they may be ignorant, undeveloped or foolish, but sinners they are not.[45] They cannot be sinners, because for him God and man are in essence one.

> The living God is a human God. Swedenborg says: God is a man, and that man is Christ. We say God is not a man, but the human in all men. God is the human power, the human element, the element which uplifts, inspires, impels forward to brighter and better futures. Man's justice is God's justice. Man's compassion is God's

---

[43] *Ibid.*, p. 19.

[44] *Ibid.*, p. 299 f.

[45] O. B. Frothingham: *The Safest Creed and Twelve Other Recent Discourses of Reason*, p. 105 f. New York: Butts, 1874.

> compassion. Man's kindness is God's kindness. When
> man forgives, God forgives. When man absolves, God
> absolves. All God's attributes are human attributes, and
> they are living as they live in us. The very unity of
> God is one with our unity. Is God one while his family
> are a thousand? Does not all the recklessness, and hate,
> and quarrel, and discord of the world break up into pieces
> our conception of the divine unity? Of course it does;
> for it suggests a kingdom divided against itself. God
> lives when man lives. God lives in the human heart;
> when the heart begins to throb and beat, his heart throbs
> and beats; and when the human heart dies, then, and
> then only, God expires.[46]

The implications of this statement stand out sharply. First,
as already indicated, the being of God is exhaustively contained in humanity. As a result, it can be said that there
is no God beyond man but that there is man or humanity
beyond God. Man is not exhaustively present in God. Second, the source of morality is man, man in his unity, so that
the essence of ethics is man's unity. Third, the unity of God
is the unity of humanity. Theological thought requires the
unity of the godhead; hence, mankind must be united. There
must be a one world order because, by definition, it is required. Fourth, any sin against the unity of man, any attempt to prevent a one world order, is a crime against humanity and therefore against God. This, of course, is the rationale
of the modern liberal, the contemporary devotee of the religion
of humanity.

As has been noted, the essence of ethics is man's unity.
This unity of humanity means mutual love irrespective of
all moral and religious factors, irrespective of anything save
the obligation to be one unified humanity. This, of course,
is a radically different concept than the Christian division
of mankind into the saved and the lost, the regenerate and
unregenerate, and the requirement of extending the second
table of the law, love of neighbor and of enemy, to all persons.
For Frothingham, "the radical's root" is this total love.[47]
This love Chase, as we have noted, advocated as having every
"magic power."[48] Earlier, a champion of Universalism,
Hosea Ballou (1771-1852) had, according to his son, "held

---

[46] *The Safest Creed*, p. 179f.
[47] *Ibid.*, pp. 45-60.
[48] Chase: *The Life-Line of the Lone One*, p. iv.

that the true way to cleanse the hardened and rebellious heart is to inundate it with a deluge of love, the only weapon of Omnipotence."[49] In these earlier forms, love was the savior and the saving power. It *changed* men; it performed the messianic role. Progressively, however, love simply came to mean the required mental attitude for the unity of humanity and did not so much *change* its object as to *sacrifice* itself to it. Practically, it meant that the "haves" gave to the "have-nots," as individuals and nations, without expecting the recipient to be transformed but simply to equalize the situation. This, of course, is "The Grand Design" of modern politics, the "transfers of capital" and goods on a vast scale. It calls for "a total transformation on a universal scale," which will, "in the non-Marxian sense at least . . . almost certainly be revolutionary."[50] Man's problem is not sin but *need*. Man is to be *"developed"* into this "divine life, not *converted* to it."[51] Men and nations are thus undeveloped rather than delinquent or evil; the answer to underdevelopment is development through the resources of the developed. It is the obligation of these developed persons and nations to contribute to the others without the foolish and interfering moralities of Christian faith.

As we have seen, Conway saw the Civil War as "revolution" and Frothingham saw it as the opportunity and means of "the reconstruction of a new order, on the basis of freedom for mankind, . . . the first installment of the Messianic Kingdom." For others, it was an unpopular war, with strong anti-abolitionist feelings and major anti-Negro, anti-abolitionist and anti-conscription rioting. But, for the abolitionists, the anti-slavery agitation was "the first installment" of world revolution and the dawn of a new day for the religion

[49] Maturin M. Ballou: *Biography of Rev. Hosea Ballou*, p. 268. Boston: Abel Tompkins, 1852.

[50] Joseph Kraft: *The Grand Design, From Common Market to Atlantic Partnership*, p. 18. New York: Harper, 1962. Walter P. Reuther, "We can make the Russians disarm," pp. 10, 14, *The Saturday Evening Post*, vol. 236, no. 43, December 7, 1963, advocates the same kind of transfer of capital and goods, calling for a $20 billion a year "long-range program of economic aid large enough to move the countries of the underdeveloped world toward a break-through into self-sustaining growth."

[51] O. B. Frothingham: *Recollections and Impressions*, 1822-1890, p. 264. New York: G. P. Putnam's Sons, 1891.

of humanity. It was the word made flesh, the new faith "made visible and palpable to all men":

> The anti-slavery agitation was felt to be something more than an attempt to apply the Beatitudes and the Parables to a flagrant case of inhumanity—it was regarded as a new interpreter of religion, a fresh declaration of the meaning of the Gospel, a living sign of the purely human character of a divine faith, an education in brotherly love and sacrifice; it was a common saying that now, for the first time in many generations, the essence of belief was made visible and palpable to all men; that Providence was teaching us in a most convincing way, and none but deaf ears could fail to understand the message.
>
> It was, indeed, a most suggestive and inspiring time. Never shall I forget, never shall I cease to be grateful for, the communion with noble minds that was brought about; the moral earnestness that was engendered, the moral insight that was quickened. Then, if ever, we ascended the Mount of Vision.[52]

The movement was especially important in that the authority of religion as the prior order to the moral sphere was emphatically denied. "It was a great experience; not only was religion brought face to face with ethics, but it was identified with ethics. It became a religion of the heart: pity, sympathy, humanity, and brotherhood were its essential principles."[53]   Instead of moral order being subordinate to and a product of theological order, the two were now identical with "the religion of the heart," with the sentimental moral impulses of the religion of humanity.

The war was exhilarating to these champions of love. Moreover, these abolitionists had to do the worst fighting, far more strenuous than the battle in the trenches.   The soldiers had "the excitement of battle, the pleasures of camp-life, the assistance of comradeship, the comfort of sympathy. The preacher (of abolition) had none of these."   Since the "whole justification" of the war "lay in its moral character," the men who fought the battle for the reconstruction of the world had the major struggle.   They had to face, moreover, in the summer of 1863 in New York "an anti-abolitionist riot, a fierce protest against the conscription, and at the same time an uprising against the government, which was

[52] *Ibid.,* p. 49 f.
[53] *Ibid.,* p. 50.

supposed to maintain a war of the blacks against the whites. The riot was directed against the negroes and the abolitionists and was pitiless and ferocious in the extreme."[54] Frothingham himself managed to reach home in safety during the first day, and, from his roof-top, watched the struggle and the entry of U.S. troops. He saw the riot as another instance of the "alliance between the despotic and the lawless," between the rulers and the masses, against true community. The deliverance of the masses lay in submission to true "Order" as represented in the dream offered by the abolitionists.[55]

Towards this end, the church should dedicate itself, to creating "a spiritual democracy." For Frothingham, the minister was not God's servant and representative, but "a representative of humanity."[56] "The coming religion" must transcend Unitarianism and Protestantism.

> The Dignity of Human Nature must be our watchword; of human *nature*, not of human *character*. For human *nature* denotes the *capacities* of man, what he *ought* to be and *shall* be, not what he *is*. Human character expresses only the undeveloped condition of man, and is therefore not to be taken as a final stand. This doctrine does not belong to a sect or a church, but to all mankind.[57]

Man will be *developed*, and "the time will come when it shall be as natural for men to do right as to breathe; when all kinds of injustice, cruelty, and tyranny will be instinctively abandoned."[58]

The religion of humanity, moreover, will approach the old forms of religion with a sophistication lacking in the early Unitarians. It will recognize the primitive grasping after truth in all the old orthodox doctrines, the doctrines of the fall, the trinity, providence and the like, as rude devices necessary for theological formulation.[59] Frothingham thus came close to formulating the neo-orthodox doctrine of myth. He also prepared the ground for the re-entrance of the religion of humanity into the churches. Unitarian, Universalist, and

---

[54] *Ibid.*, p. 106 f.
[55] *Ibid.*, p. 112 f.
[56] *Ibid.*, pp. 116, 150.
[57] *Ibid.*, p. 285.
[58] *Ibid.*, p. 286 f.
[59] *Religion of Humanity*, p. 319 f.

Spiritualist churches had begun by withdrawing from evangelical Christianity, confident that the people would quickly follow them. The exception to this was New England, where the existing Congregationalist churches were often taken over and the orthodox members ousted. Although these groups established churches throughout the United States, there was no general exodus into them, and it was quickly obvious, to Frothingham as to others, that the American people as a whole intended to remain faithful to orthodox Christianity.

The strategy after the Civil War therefore changed markedly. There was less attempt made to draw the people and more to win the clergy. Previously, church conflict had been over Calvinism versus Arminianism, over liberalism, with major divisions resulting. Subsequently, this ceased to be a major issue and was almost non-existent, except mainly for the Machen controversy over liberalism in the Presbyterian Church U.S.A., and the H. Hoeksema common grace division from the Christian Reformed Church, both having their origin in the 1920's. The issues ceased to be primarily *theological;* the church now faced a battle for its very existence as in any sense an institution of historic Christianity. On the whole, the battle was lost, or is being lost, in virtually every major branch of the church. Modernism and the social gospel triumphed, expressions of the religion of humanity, as are neo-orthodoxy and existentialism.[60]

The ramifications of the social gospel movement are best seen by examining its leadership, as given by Robert T. Handy of Union Theological Seminary. In France, the Christian social movement (called in some places Christian Socialism, in others the social gospel) had as its leaders H. F. R. Lamennais and C. H. Saint-Simon; in Italy, Guiseppe Mazzini; Hermann Kutter and Leonhard Ragaz in Switzerland; Friedrich Naumann and Adolf von Harnack in Germany; in England, Maurice and Kingsley, followed by Ruskin, Headlam, Holland, and Gore; in the United States, Washington Gladden, Graham Taylor, George D. Herron, William D. P. Bliss, and

---

[60] See J. Gresham Machen: *Christianity and Liberalism:* Grand Rapids: Eerdmans, 1946; Cornelius Van Til: *Christianity and Barthianism,* Philadelphia: Presbyterian and Reformed, 1962. Machen, p. 8, saw liberalism as "a return to an un-Christian and a sub-Christian form of the religious life."

Walter Rauschenbusch.[61] It is not our purpose here to consider the history of the social gospel movement. This has been extensively treated in a number of works from various perspectives. It was in essence the capture of the churches by the forces of the religion of humanity and was another and more radical Babylonian captivity of the church. In 1869, Frothingham had dreamed of the new order, of "The Church of the Future, incarnating the Religion of Humanity," to use Phillips' phrase, which would create the new society:

> Thus we dream of society. There is no society now. There is at present no such thing as society. Society means brotherhood, good-will, sociability, mutual love, mutual fancy, mutual purpose, and achievement. There is no such thing now. It is a fancy; it is a dream; it lies far off in the very remote future. . . We have not, as yet, felt out how the law upon which society can be built. The best reformers, the finest economists, the noblest teachers in social sciences are just now getting hold of the threads by which we shall be conducted at last into the new paradise.[62]

The champions of the social gospel set out to conduct men "into the new paradise." They were now men who spoke from the pulpits of evangelical Christianity and in the name of the historic faith. What was their message?

One of the triumphs of the religion of humanity was the World's Congress of Religions, August 25 to October 15, 1893, at the World's Columbian Exposition, in Chicago. At this Congress, Judaism, Hinduism, Buddhism, Confucianism, Shintoism and Mohammedanism, as well as other religions, shared the stage with Christianity as equally valid. The published papers of the Congress bore, on the title page, Pope's words:

> For modes of faith let graceless zealots fight;
> He can't be wrong, whose life is in the right.

Theology is nothing, and ethics is everything, with true ethics being the ethics of the religion of humanity. As the Congregationalist, Rev. Lyman Abbott (1835-1922), expressed it,

[61] Robert T. Handy, "Social Gospel," in L. A. Loetscher, ed.: *Twentieth Century Encyclopedia of Religious Knowledge*, an Extension of *The New Schaff-Herzog Encyclopedia of Religious Knowledge*, vol. ii, p. 1036f.

[62] Frothingham: *The Foes of Society*, p. 6 cited in Phillips: *Puritan and Unitarian Views*, p. L9.

"Religion is the mother of all religions, not the child." This essential religion is non-theological and is a capacity native to man. Properly developed, it led to "a united race," humanity united. Man was born out of unity, God, and must return to unity. "God made us out of Himself and God calls us back to Himself." God has spoken in all religions but supremely in Christ, the "prophet" of the Golden Rule and the great moral teacher. He provides for the "universal hunger of the human race" for "a better understanding of our moral relations, one to another."[63] The Rev. E. L. Rexford of Boston sounded a major note of the Congress, a plea for the solidarity of the human race and for total religious unity.[64] Rev. William R. Alger of New York looked ahead to the unification of the human race and charted the steps. First,

----

[63] Lyman Abbott, "Religion Essentially Characteristic of Humanity," in J. W. Hanson, ed.: *The World's Congress of Religions, Addresses and Papers*, pp. 640-649. Chicago: International Publishing Co., 1894. The Congress was regarded with disfavor or ignored by most of the strict believers of all religions, but hailed with delight by the liberals of all groups. Thus, the liberal American Jews reported, "When the idea of holding a Parliament of all Religions in connection with the World's Fair of Chicago was broached there was no denomination that hailed it with greater enthusiasm than the Jewish," p. iii, *Judaism at the World's Parliament of Religions*, published by the Union of American Hebrew Congregations; Cincinnati: Robert Clarke, 1894. Each faith saw itself as an important forerunner of the one universal religion. Since then, the idea of the unity of all religions has been infiltrating into some evangelical circles, eroding the older emphasis on the uniqueness and integrity of the Christian faith. Thus, Billy Graham, in his revivalism is said to refer people to the *church* (Roman Catholic or Protestant, Modernist or evangelical) or *synagogue* of their own choice, thereby clearly indicating his divergence from Christian orthodoxy; see Cleveland Amory, "Celebrity Register," in *McCall's Magazine*, vol. XCI, no. no. 5, February, 1964, p. 62. Such a procedure is not new to American revivalism which is by no means to be associated with historic orthodoxy. A defender of Graham has written of evangelist Billy Sunday: "The truth is that when Sunday concluded the New York campaign, 3,690 cards were sent to the Roman Catholic church, 803 were sent to Hebrew synagogues (and 497 to Christian Science churches) in addition to all the other churches who received cards bearing the inquirers' names. Mr. Graham is much more careful in such matters. During the New York Crusade, in spite of the accusations of uninformed critics, not one card was knowingly sent to these types of churches." Robert O. Ferm: *Cooperative Evangelism, Is Billy Graham Right or Wrong?*, p. 84. Grand Rapids: Zondervan, 1958.

[64] E. L. Rexford, "The Religious Intent," *Congress Papers*, pp. 651-657.

there would be a partial unification through aesthetic unification. Second, is scientific unification, and "third is the essential," which he did not define. Fourth comes "the political unification by the establishment of an international code for the settlement of all disputes by reason," and fifth, "the commercial and social, the free circulation of all component items of humanity through the whole of humanity." Redemption is social and "must be realized on earth." Moreover, Christ is more than the individual, Jesus of Nazareth:

> He is the completed genus incarnate. He is the absolute generic unity of the human race in manifestation. Therefore, he is not the follower of other men, but their divine exemplar. We must not limit our worship of Christ to the mere historic person, but must see in the individual person the perfected genus of the divine humanity which is God Himself, and realize that that is to be multiplied. It cannot be divided, but it may be multiplied commensurately with the dimensions of the whole human race.[65]

In other words, we are all to become Christs.

The economic question was, of course, dealt with, the Rev. Washington Gladden (originally Solomon Washington, 1836-1918) a Congregationalist, calling for a Christian distribution of wealth.

> If the function of wealth under the divine order is the development of manhood, then it is plain that an equal distribution of it would be altogether inadmissible; for under such a distribution some would obtain far less than they could use with benefit and others far more.

> The Socialistic maxims: "To each according to his needs," and "To each according to his worth," are evidently ambiguous. What needs? The needs of the body or of the spirit? And how can we assure ourselves that by any distribution which we could effect real needs would be supplied? Any distribution according to the supposed needs would be constantly perverted? It is impossible for us to ascertain and measure the real needs of men.

> "To each according to his works" is equally uncertain. What works? Works of greed or works of love? Works whose aim is sordid or works whose aim is social? According to the divine plan the function of wealth, as we have seen, is the perfection of character and the

---

[65] William R. Alger, "The Only Possible Method of Religious Unification of the Human Race," *Congress Papers*, pp. 253-256.

promotion of social welfare. The divine plan must, therefore, be that wealth shall be so distributed as to secure
the greatest results. And religion, which seeks to discern
and follow the divine plan, must teach that the wealth
of the world will be rightly distributed, only when every
man shall have as much as he can wisely use to make
himself a better man, and the community in which he
lives a better community; so much and no more.[66]

It is apparent that these men could declare that they were
not Marxists. The dissent is real, but the revolutionary faith
is even more apparent. Wealth must be distributed, but since
true needs vary, the distribution must vary. Who can determine what constitutes true needs? Who shall say, "So much
and no more"? Obviously, a spiritual elite. Gladden and
his followers saw the state as the agency of distribution and
a spiritual elite as the men who "discern and follow the
divine plan." Gladden, Lymen Abbott, and others paved the
way for the ostensible trust-busting of Theodore Roosevelt.[67]
An Englishman, W. T. Stead of London, proposed a "Civic
Church," a kind of council of churches, social agencies, and
public welfare minded atheists to serve as an establishment
for "the progressive development of a more perfect social
system."[68]

Prof. F. G. Peabody of Harvard also discussed "the social
question," stating that Jesus was not only "the great individu-
alist of history" but also "the great socialist as well."

Individualism means self-culture, self-interest, self-
development. Socialism means self-sacrifice, self-forget-
fulness, the public good. Christ means both. Cultivate
yourself, He says, make the most of yourself, enrich
yourself, and then take it all and make it the instrument
of self-sacrifice. Give the perfect developed self to the
perfect common good. The only permanent socialism
must be based on perfected individualism. The kingdom
of God is not to come of itself; it is to come through
the collective consecration of individual souls.[69]

For this facile and sterile rationalism, all the values of the

---

[66] Washington Gladden, *"Religion and Wealth,"* Congress Papers,
p. 838.

[67] Robert R. Roberts, "The Social Gospel and the Trust-Busters,"
Church History, vol. 25, pp. 239-257, September, 1956.

[68] W. T. Stead, "The Civic Church," *Congress Papers*, pp. 763-772.

[69] F. G. Peabody, "Christianity and the Social Question," *Congress Papers*, p. 908f.

past would remain as a kind of biological inheritance for the planners of the united humanity to make use of.

In 1910, when the Baptist, Rev. Walter Rauschenbusch (1861-1918), spoke to the Berlin Congress of Free Christianity, he had cause to rejoice in the progress of the social gospel in the United States. The Federal Council of Churches had been established in 1908, socialism was coalescing with Christianity; prohibition and women's suffrage were progressing. He could thus hope that "the movement towards Socialism, which must be recognized as historically inevitable, might not be a class movement, but a movement of the people."[70]

A second Parliament of Religions was held in Chicago, in connection with the Chicago Fair, in 1933. The Rev. Jabez T. Sunderland, Billings Lecturer of the American Unitarian Association to the Far East and active in the 1893 Congress, spoke of the practical results of that first meeting. Among the notable accomplishments, he cited the establishment of chairs of Comparative Religion in many universities and theological schools in America, and the broadening of the scope of foreign missions towards a sympathy for the "good in other faiths." The Congress had thus exercised a leavening influence.[71] The ultimate ideal of a world religion was presented by various persons, including Rabbi Julian Morgenstern, president of Hebrew Union College, while the Unitarian Dean Curtis W. Reese called for a planned and classless society.[72] John Dewey was also a speaker, calling for a new politics, because the fundamental problem of the day was not the fact of man's sinful state but "the system under

---

[70] W. Rauschenbusch, "The Social Awakening in the Churches of America," in Charles W. Wendt, ed.: *Fifth International Congress of Free Christianity and Religious Progress, Berlin, August 5-10, 1910,* p. 567. Berlin, 1911. An aspect of the social gospel and religion of humanity movement, which deserves study is the extensive subsidy of such literature. Rauschenbusch's *Christianizing the Social Order* (New York: Macmillan, 1913) was in 1913 and possibly later distributed freely to seminary students, with a mimeographed note from Rauschenbusch, under a subsidy from a "generous giver."

[71] Jabez T. Sunderland, "The Two World Parliaments of Religion— 1893 and 1933," in Charles Frederick Weller, ed.: *World Fellowship, Addresses and Messages by Leading Spokesmen of All Faiths, Races and Countries,* pp. 512-523. New York: Liveright, 1935.

[72] Julian Morgenstern, "Nationalism, Universalism, and World-Religion," pp. 59-67; Curtis W. Reese, "Introduction to a Planned Society," pp. 97-102, *World Fellowship.*

which we live."[73]   Bishop William Montgomery Brown of
Galion, Ohio, called for "communism, whatever its cost," as
"a human necessity." "We must banish gods from the skies
and capitalists from the earth in order to make way for united
human life, world communism."[74]   Carl D. Thompson, secretary of the Public Ownership League of America, saw public
ownership as "the way out." Mrs. Charlotte Perkins Gilman
saw "the end of senseless sin and shame" and the dawn of
true consciousness in a one-world order. The individual as
such is not real; he is a "constituent part," a unit in the whole.

> Humanity is not a species of animal; it is an organic
> relationship in which the individual is a constituent part.
> A Society is the unit of humanity. A solitary human
> being is a contradiction in terms. The nearer we trace
> savagery back to mere pairing, or to the loose horde,
> the less humanity is seen. Humanity is a new stage of
> life. It appears in social relationship and develops with
> it. We are as yet but partially human.[75]

Man, in short, is only man en masse, as a member of humanity. He derives his identity, in this faith, not from God but
from humanity. It follows, therefore, that since his identity
and true being is in union with humanity, his salvation rests
in unified humanity. This clearly was the faith of the religion
of humanity.

A number of institutions were created to further this
faith, notably the Federal Council of the Churches of Christ
in America, established in 1908 and, in 1950, merging with
seven interdenominational functional agencies to create the
National Council of the Churches of Christ in the U.S.A.
The purpose and interest of the Federal Council was neither
theological nor evangelical but rather social, and at its inception, it adopted a statement on the "Social Ideals of the
Churches." An expanded and developed statement of these
social gospel principles was adopted on December 8, 1932.
In 1911, Charles S. Macfarland was made acting executive
secretary of the Council. Macfarland had no hesitation about

---

[73] John Dewey, "Needed—A New Politics," in *World Fellowship*,
p. 124.
[74] William Montgomery Brown, "Communism—The New Faith for
a New World," *World Fellowship*, p. 176.
[75] C. P. Gilman, "The Social Body and Soul," *World Fellowship*,
p. 259.

emphasizing the social gospel. Both unity and the social gospel were the gospel of Jesus.

> Jesus imparted to his disciples the spirit of unity, with profound underlying principles of truth and life which were to preserve it. His teaching also gives us the basis of a social gospel, which as we shall see, implies and necessitates Christian unity. Inasmuch as the social implications of the gospel of Jesus have been so largely the objectives of modern movements of unity, it is important to realize their significance. His constant use of the term "Kingdom of Heaven" implies what we now term the "social order," with its spiritual and Christian meaning. Jesus rescued the individual from the unsocial institutionalism of his day and, by his lofty evaluation of personality, instituted a new social ideal, for social redemption is, above all, the freeing of personality.[76]

The Federal Council created various subordinate and coordinate agencies which in themselves became vast enterprises. Church World Service, for example, whose functions were essentially humanitarian, during World War II and after handled nearly $50,000,000 of overseas aid in money, clothing, food, and medical supplies.

The Federal Council was succeeded in 1950 by the National Council of the Churches of Christ in the United States of America, a body which included the Federal Council and seven other interdenominational bodies. Under the new title, there was no abatement of the old faith but its intensification. Ecumenical activities were also fostered, and the United Nations seen as a noble cause. Earlier, the Federal Council had approved the U.N. Charter "within 24 hours after the close of the United Nations Conference on International Organization at San Francisco" in 1945. It spoke of "the humanitarian aims set forth in the preamble," and declared that "The will to cooperate requires as a foundation, a new international morality. Without this, the structure of the peace will rest on shifting sand." The churches must "establish a strong core of world-minded Christians" as its "inescapable duty," to the end "that all of the family of nations may come to work together in harmony."[77]

---

[76] Charles S. Macfarland: *Christian Unity in Practice and Prophecy*, p. 14. New York: Macmillan, 1933. For the text of the "Social Ideals," see pp. 294-315.

[77] *Christian Century*, July 11, 1945, p. 818, "Federal Council Approves Charter."

In 1946, the World Council of Churches sought "a special relationship" with the United Nations, and the World Council of Christians and Jews had its bid for affiliation with UNESCO approved by the U.S. State Department.[78] In a short time, the Commission of the Churches on International Affairs was admitted to consultative status at the U.N. Council.[79]

In the summer of 1946, a conference of church leaders, authorized by the World Council of Churches and the International Missionary Council, met in Cambridge, England to adopt a charter for the Commission of the Churches on International Affairs whose preamble contained a very remarkable sentence: "The Church as God purposes it is a unique community of men without boundaries of nation or race, culture or tradition—unconditional unity grounded in the unconditional love of God."[80] No plainer denial of orthodox Christianity can be made. "Unconditional unity" is a denial of the fact that biblical unity requires true faith in Jesus Christ, and an obedience to His word, as its first premise. Unity in Christianity must be conditional. "The unconditional love of God" is again a myth of the religion of humanity. Until man finds atonement in and through the saving, vicarious sacrifice of Jesus Christ, man is, according to the Scriptures, under the wrath and the law of God. The love of God is conditional, and to speak of an unconditional love of God for man is to deny the biblical faith. It is to assert that God loves all men equally, so that a man's faith and its works are without standing in the sight of God, since the unregenerate and regenerate are equally objects of His love. Nor is the love of God unconditional towards believers, for the Bible gives clear-cut evidence of the anger of God towards many a saint, including Moses, David and Hezekiah. The unity of the church is similarly conditional upon true faith and obedience. The perspective of this charter is not Christianity, but the religion of human-

---

[78] *Facts on File Yearbook* 1946, vol. VI, p. 250 c, 72 c, 108 e. New York: Peterson's Index.

[79] *United Nations Yearbook*, 1947-1948, p. 694; 1948-1949, pp. 119, 711, 694.

[80] Paul Griswold Macy: *If It Be Of God*, p. 90. St. Louis: Bethany Press, 1960. The author is here indebted to C. L. Apple for calling his attention to this and similar materials.

ity, for it seeks, not the glory of God but "the benefit of mankind." In referring to the ecumenical movement, the preamble declared, "This brotherly unity which God has given and blessed will surely be further strengthened if we acknowledged our obligation to use it for the benefit of mankind."

Very soon, the Commission of the Churches on International Affairs (CCIA) could report that "Judgments from impartial sources credit the CCIA with making a substantial contribution to the drafting and adoption of the Universal Declaration of Human Rights, especially with respect to the provision for religious freedom and the rights closely related thereto."[81]

The rise of neo-orthodoxy made no difference to the progress of the religion of humanity except to clothe it more than ever in the traditional language of Christianity. Neo-orthodoxy was, after all, to use Van Til's description, simply "the new modernism," more radical than the old in its theology as well as its sociology.

The social gospel was now the faith of most churches and the teaching of most of the major seminaries. Its teachings were in essence and temper alien to orthodox Christianity. First of all, the social gospel assumes as an article of faith the evolutionary dogma. As a result, the basic fact of history is development, not creation, the fall, and the regeneration of man through Jesus Christ. Second, the social gospel asserts the primacy of the moral order to theological order. Although neo-orthodox sophistication would appear to deny this, the essence of Barth's god is that he underwrites the autonomy of man by his freedom. This ethics, being evolutionary, is grounded on the idea of development rather than regeneration. As a result, ethics stems from human needs and necessities rather than from the divine decree. Since human need governs ethics, it is asserted increasingly that, because we are under love, not law, "Thou shalt not commit adultery" admits at the very least some exceptions in the name of love. If the sexual relation is personal, an I—thou affair rather than impersonal, I—it, Martin Buber's language being commonly used here, it is holy and legiti-

---

[81] *1947-49 Report, The Commission of the Churches on International Affairs,* p. 10.

mate.[82]   This is echoed from many pulpits.   In Canada, when
Pierre Burton was fired by *Maclean's* Magazine for offering
a similar position, he was asked to write a Lenten study book
by the Canadian Anglican Church.[83]

Third, because the social gospel is all-inclusive in its
conception of acceptability to God, almost the only unpardon-
able sin and heresy is Christian orthodoxy.   Fourth, being
evolutionary, it assumes the past as a part of its inheritance,
like biological data, an accomplished fact, and it fails to realize that it is itself a destructive force, rapidly eroding the
inheritance it assumes as fixed.   Fifth, it sees sin in the
system, not in man.   While talking more of sin now than
in the past, the social gospel still sees sin as basically social
rather than personal.   Sixth, as a result, salvation must be
social also, and it requires the re-ordering of society.   Seventh,
its view of man is therefore basically that man is a social
animal rather than a creature of God.   As we have seen, man
is defined in terms of humanity rather than the Creator.
Eighth, man's "mental health," a substitute concept for sin,
is also determined by his orientation to humanity.   For such
men as Dr. H. A. Overstreet and Dr. Brock Chisholm, mental
sickness means resistance to the social gospel and one-world-
ism.[84]   As a result, what begins by asserting the primacy
of ethics to theology ends up by denying ethics as well.   The
modern mental health movement would substitute, for law,
in theory and in practice, the concept of sickness, or disease
for sin, so that law enforcement would pass from the people
and their representatives to medical experts.   The moral basis
of crime is denied, and the historic Christian foundation of

---

[82] See William Graham Cole: *Called to Responsible Freedom: The
Meaning of Sex in the Christian Life*, National Council of the Churches
of Christ in the U.S.A., New York: 1961.

[83] See "Collector's Item for Lent," *Christianity Today*, p. 36f., vol.
VIII, no. 10, Feb. 14, 1964.

[84] See Brock Chisholm: *Prescription for Survival*, New York:
Columbia, 1957; and H. A. Overstreet: *The Great Enterprise, Relating
Ourselves to Our World;* New York: Norton, 1952.   Chisholm holds
strict religious orthodoxy to be a major factor in "mental illness," and,
for him, it must be so by definition.   Chisholm does admit that psychiatry has "done practically nothing for the patient," and that psychiatrists are largely moved by "a sense of power over other people's lives."
Chisholm is a Unitarian; Lisa Hobbs, "An Eminent Psychiatrist Tells
Why His Science is Oversold," in *People, The California Weekly*, Sunday, December 22, 1963, p. 5; *S. F. Examiner.*

law subverted. Dr. Edward Glover, co-founder of the Institute for the Study and Treatment of Delinquency, sees as one of the great potential accomplishments of the 20th century the emancipation of law and sociology from "moralistic conceptions of crime."[85]

This change, however, was well under way in the early part of the century. An especially dramatic and sordid crime, the murder of Robert Franks on May 21, 1924, by Richard Loeb and Nathan Leopold, was made occasion for the promulgation of this new concept. Clarence Darrow assumed their defense, on a plea of guilty, seeking to avert execution on the ground that the punishment of crime was a barbaric concept. "Hatred only causes hatred." The answer is love: "Soften this human heart . . . through charity, and love and understanding."[86] Darrow's final word was an affirmation of the gospel of love, with Omar Khayyam quoted as an ideal for all:

So I be written in the Book of Love,
I do not care about that Book above.
Erase my name or write it as you will,
So I be written in the Book of Love.

Darrow dared claim Jesus for this gospel of indiscriminate love, holding it would be "blasphemy to say" that Leopold and Loeb would not "be safe in the hands of the founder of the Christian religion."[87]

This gospel of undiscriminating love has three implications. First, it gives tacit assent to evil by accepting it without anger, judgment or hate. Hate, according to the Scriptures, clearly has a healthy and God-given place (Heb.

[85] See T. Robert Ingram, ed.: *Essays on The Death Penalty*, p. 88. Houston: St. Thomas Press, 1963. The names of prisons are being changed in terms of this new "medical" approach; thus, in California, there are such institutions as the Soledad Correctional Facility.

[86] *The Plea of Clarence Darrow, August 22nd, 23rd and 25th, 1924, In Defense of Richard Loeb and Nathan Leopold Jr. on Trial for Murder*, p. 50. Authorized and Revised Edition. Chicago: Ralph Fletcher Seymour.

[87] Darrow, p. 51. This religion of humanity, with salvation by love, is common to many religions today wherever the new forces have taken over. Thus, in *The Burning Bush*, Issue Number One, Summer, 1963 (5723), The Inter-Hillel Council of Northern California, San Francisco, Leland S. Meyerzove, in "Sefer Ari," wrote, "For when we all return to love we shall be in Eden," p. 34.

1:9; Ps. 34:16; 98:10; Proverbs 8:13; Ps. 139:21,22; etc.), as does love. Indeed, as Spurgeon pointed out, hatred between the godly and the ungodly is God's first blessing after the fall, Gen. 3:15. Both love and hate, when exercised in violation of God's law, can be evil, even as both under God can be holy. Only God is unconditionally good. Second, the gospel of love is a denial of justice, since it affirms either its irrelevance or asserts love to be a higher way than justice. Third, there can be no denial of justice without a corresponding denial of responsibility. The biblical concept of law and justice rests on the premise of man's responsibility and accountability. The gospel of love says that man's sins are due, not to his fallen nature, but a lack in his being which love can supply, aided, of course, by psychiatry and medicine. Man must be loved in his sin because sin and crime are not man's fault.

Clarence Darrow based his case on this doctrine of irresponsibility and love. "They killed him because they were made that way." They are not, he insisted, "to blame for it."[88] Nature, not the boys, is at fault, because Nature made them that way:

> Is Dickey Loeb to blame because out of the infinite forces that conspired to form him, the infinite forces that were at work producing him ages before he was born, that because out of these infinite combinations he was born without it? (i.e., without "emotional feelings") If he is, then there should be a new definition for justice. Is he to blame for what he did not have and never had? Is he to blame that his machine is imperfect? Who is to blame? I do not know. I have never in my life been interested so much in fixing blame as I have in relieving people from blame. I am not wise enough to fix it. I know that somewhere in the past that entered into him something missed. It may be defective nerves. It may be a defective heart or liver. It may be defective endocrine glands. I know it is something. I know that nothing happens in this world without a cause.[89]

The meaning is obvious. Crime is an obsolete concept. Crimes spring, not from evil in the heart of man, but from a faulty biological inheritance. Can we condemn a man because he was born with "a defective heart or liver?" Can

---

[88] *Ibid.,* p. 27.
[89] *Ibid.,* p. 55.

we condemn a man for perversion, or for murder, if he acts out of his own biology? The real criminal is Nature, if we are in search of one. "Nature is strong and she is pitiless. She works in her own mysterious way, and we are her victims."[90] As a result, Darrow could ask, "What had this boy to do with it? . . . All of this was handed to him. . . He did not make himself. And yet he is compelled to pay."[91] To think otherwise is "crazy." There are only two possibilities. "I know that one of two things happened to Richard Loeb; that this terrible crime was inherent in his organism, and came from some ancestor, or that it came through his education and his training after he was born. Do I need to prove it?"[92] It was in brief, either heredity or environment, not the man. But Darrow did not hesitate to accuse the defense of a lust for blood and did not excuse them on either ground!

Darrow, as a materialist, was not sure that a mind existed in man. "The mind, of course, is an illusive thing. Whether it exists or not no one can tell."[93] Nature itself is governed by chance, and everything depends, not on responsibility, but "on infinite chances." "Their parents happened to meet, these boys happened to meet; some sort of chemical alchemy operated so that they cared for each other, and poor Bobby Frank's dead body was found in the culvert as a result."[94]

Darrow used one theory after another to vindicate irresponsibility and enthrone biology and medicine in place of law. Crime was immaturity, biological immaturity. It meant living in a world of delusions. "There could be no childhood without delusions,"[95] and many people retained childish delusions into mature years. This is a psychiatric rather than legal problem. The need is for *treatment*, not punishment. "It never occurs to the lawyer that crime has a cause as certainly as disease, and that the way to rationally treat any abnormal condition is to remove the cause."[96] For Darrow, as a materialist, the world was impersonal, and hence *causality* is by definition impersonal. For a Christian, the world

[90] *Ibid.*, p. 70.
[91] *Ibid.*, p. 71.
[92] Ibid., p. 73.
[93] *Ibid.*, p. 61.
[94] *Ibid.*, p. 87.
[95] *Ibid.*, p. 67.
[96] *Ibid.*, p. 104.

is the personal act of a personal God, and hence causality, human and divine, is personal. Thus, in crime, "to remove the cause" is to remove the person, in murder, by execution. This Darrow refused to consider.

Darrow's thesis has many adherents today in law, especially among judges. It has its champions elsewhere also, notably among the liberal clergy, since it is an article of faith in the religion of humanity. Another adherent, apparently, is Nathan Leopold.

> In applying for parole Leopold reminded the board that biologically, not one cell in his body was the same, 33 years later, as when he committed the crime. He had described himself as an "insufferable creature" then, "a creature I hope I have long since ceased to be." All he could do, he wrote, was continue to try to atone in his daily life for the crime he had committed as a boy.[97]

In this perspective, therefore, man's basic problem, and the cause of his criminality and sin, is the biological limitation of his being. "The human situation is one of finiteness," according to Tillich."[98] For neo-orthodoxy, *finitude* is man's basic problem. Finitude is creatureliness, and, for the orthodox Christian, this is not a problem but his God-given situation. The problem is his moral rebellion against God and his attempt to be as God, to try to transcend his creatureliness and finiteness. It is possible to speak of sin, and Tillich and Niebuhr do so at length, but an idea of sin conditioned by the belief that finiteness is a problem for man is ultimately a denial of the biblical doctrine of sin. The remedy for sin, in this perspective, is social and medical action. In this perspective, man begins by trying to be more than man and ends up by running from the responsibility of manhood.

In this perspective too, liberty is not "under God" but under the state, since man is a creature of the state. Thus, the United Nations' Universal Declaration of Human Rights is a statist document. The liberties it affirms are given by the state and subject to arbitrary revocation by the state authorities. The state thus has total jurisdiction over the

---

[97] Leonard Lyons, "The rehabilitation of Nathan Leopold," *The Saturday Evening Post*, June 1, 1963, vol. 236, no. 21, p. 67. Lyons reported that in the library of his home Leopold had the framed photo of Richard Loeb.

[98] Paul Tillich: *The Shaking of the Foundations*, p. 17 New York: Scribner, 1948.

life of man and can remove every "right" from him at will. In Crocker's words, the "Universal Declaration" is "a sham, a wordy invitation to tyranny."[99]

Thus, the religion of humanity, by the 1960's, had become not only the religion of most churches, preached from pulpits, and resounding from papal encyclical and from world church groups, but it was in effect the established religion of the courts and of most states the world over. It was also the implicitly established faith of the United Nations. Not without some popular following, it has nevertheless met with extensive grass-roots resistance, especially in the United States, but its power on the top is very great. By its omnipresence in most news and communications media, and its presence in church and state, it is working to weaken the moral fiber of the people. Pasteur's words were apt: "the microbe is nothing, the *terrain* is everything." Every attempt is being made, in and through the schools and other media, to create that favorable terrain. The terrain, here, however, is *man,* created in the image of God, and man, though fallen, is ethically, not metaphysically separated from God. His nature remains the same, a creature of God, made in His image and responsible to Him, made under God's law and made to obey Him. Man can alienate himself morally to his own destruction, but he cannot alienate himself metaphysically. He remains always a creature of God; he cannot become a creature of the state or of man. The religion of humanity is therefore a delusion which can only destroy those who put their trust in it.

Meanwhile, President L. B. Johnson has called for the erection of a church in Washington, D.C., dedicated to the common use of all faiths, as "a fitting memorial to the God who made us all." The president's use of the word "memorial" was ironically fitting; the god of this faith is dead; what is important to it is the union or common action of "religious groups of all faiths."[100]

Meanwhile too a new concept of religious liberty is increasingly proclaimed, perhaps most clearly stated by an articulate voice of the religion of humanity:

---

[99] George Crocker, "U. N. Human Rights," *S. F. Examiner,* Sunday, December 15, 1963, Sec. III, p. 4.

[100] "Johnson Urges 'Memorial to God,' " Palo Alto, California, *Times* Wednesday, February 5, 1964, p. 1.

> . . . true religious freedom, to which our nation is dedi-
> cated, comes in two distinct parts: freedom *of* and *from*
> religion. (And your "freedom for religion" is more a
> matter of the former than the latter.) "Freedom of"
> assures us that our government will not interfere with
> our religion; "freedom from" guarantees us that our re-
> ligion will not interfere with our government. In order
> to have a true separation of church and state, we must
> have both kinds of freedom. At present we have only
> freedom of religion (relatively speaking); we do not
> have freedom from it. Examples of religion's involve-
> ment in government include our so-called Blue Laws, and
> the statutes concerning sex behavior, divorce, birth con-
> trol, abortion, censorship, etc., in many of our states, as
> well as a certain number of the local executive and judic-
> ial decisions related to these same subjects.[101]

What is here asked is a contradiction. There can be no freedom *for* religion if there is a strict legal requirement also
of freedom *from* religion. This would mean that a religion
can have little existence outside the mind of the believer. No
group of believers can order society, if in the majority, to
their ideal concept of law. But this is not quite what is
desired. The older forms of religion, and in the United States
this means orthodox Christianity, cannot have any right to
continue their legal structuring of society or to develop it,
for *only the religion of humanity is granted the right to effect
legislation.* Thus, in the name of religious liberty, we have
a denial of religious liberty to all groups save the religion
of humanity. Whenever the Church of Rome has at times,
in certain states, worked to maintain an order permitting
religious liberty to all if all are Roman Catholics, the liberal
hue and cry has been great. Now, in the name of religious
liberty, the religion of humanity asserts precisely this and
calls it a new freedom for man. There is liberty for all,
but only to practice the religion of humanity.

This new order cannot tolerate Christian orthodoxy, for
it regards "Good" and "Evil" as "two concepts so alien to
the needs of the age, inaccessible to reasoning logic, with

---

[101] "Freedom From Religion," in *Playboy*, vol. 10, no. 10, October,
1963, p. 70. For a minister's hearty approval of *Playboy*, see pp. 73f. of
the same number. *Playboy's* philosophy advocates a new legal structure,
one in line with the religion of humanity on the whole, and it is not
surprising that a major Western university should have its bound volumes of *Playboy* in its law library.

their claims to eternal validity."[102]   Men must live beyond
God and beyond good and evil. It means saying "yea" to
all of life. "Any 'nay' indicates the presence of some evil."[103]
"To live happily: aware that he owes his life to no one,
nor needs any pretext for living. To live happily—that
means: ridding oneself of the shame of imperfection."[104]
Significantly enough, this life beyond God and ethics means
also "assuming responsibility . . . . Responsibility for your
life, all life, any life."[105] Having denied God and moral law,
man can then assume total responsibility for "all life, any
life."

But, to achieve this, any law above and beyond man
must be denied, even as God is denied, in the name of man's
sovereignty. Thus, The Committee for Personal Freedom
seeks the abolition of all religious and moral influence on
legislation and freedom for every kind of sexual activity.[106]
There is a similar goal in much organized homosexual activity.[107] Pornography is seen as a valuable social tool in breaking down "impotence and frigidity" caused by religious restrictions and hence "as of redeeming social importance."[108] It is in line with this that an article in a National Council of Churches periodical urged, as against "the
older, discredited historical myth" a new faith, like unto "our
rediscovery of Israel's lost earth and the lost divinities of
that earth. Once again we have come in contact with those
powers of life and death which engendered men's feelings

---

[102] Kurt R. Grossman, ed.: Michael Wurmbrand, *The Man and His Work*, p. 115. New York: Philosophical Library, 1956.

[103] *Ibid.*, p. 120.

[104] *Ibid.*, p. 116.

[105] *Ibid.*, p. 85. Grossman says of Wurmbrand, "Of Michael Wurm-brand you can truly say: Ecce Homo. (Behold the man)," p. 34.

[106] Michael Leigh: *The Velvet Underground*, pp. 176 ff.

[107] R. E. L. Masters: *The Homosexual Revolution.* A Challenging Expose of the social and political directions of a minority group. New York: Julian Press, 1962. For the possibility that "civil rights" for homosexuals as a cause "partly replacing the Negro as an object of liberal solicitude and the prime test of liberal tolerance," see Dennis H. Wrong, "Homosexuality in America," in *New Society*, (No. 29), 27 June 1963, p. 19.

[108] Stanley Edgar Hyman, "In Defense of Pornography," in *The New Leader*, vol. XLVI, no. 18, September 2, 1963, pp. 13-15. See also "An Interview with Dr. Albert Ellis," in *The Campus Voice*, issue 19, pp. 6-11.

about Baal, Astarte, and Anath.   These powers have again become decisive in our religious life."[109]   In keeping with this revival of the fertility cult faith is the declaration by a professor in a church related college "that the act of intercourse is itself to serve as an outward and visible symbol of communion, not merely between man and wife but with God."[110]

Like instances can be multiplied at great length.   Suffice it to note that the religion of humanity is the established religion of most of the courts of law, of the schools, colleges and universities, of the hierarchies of most churches, and of great numbers of the peoples of the West.   The Christian resistance, however, is greater than is normally recognized, and it is increasing.

---

[109] Richard L. Rubenstein, "Person and Myth in the Judaeo-Christian Encounter," in *Christian Scholar*, XLVI, 4, Winter, 1963, p. 284.

[110] Robert H. Bonthuis: *Christian Paths to Self-Acceptance*, p. 213 f. New York King's Crown Press, 1948, 1952.

Chapter VII

THE UNITED NATIONS

Any discussion of the United Nations is inevitably a religious discussion, for the principles which that organization embodies are not merely political and economic but inescapably religious. As a result, an historical study, however valuable in its own sphere, is inappropriate to our concern. The failures of the U.N. are real and they are many, but it can perhaps be legitimately argued that, as a young institution, it needs time to mature and that its errors are the accidents of youth rather than the diseases of old age. The more basic question is this: Is it established on a solid foundation, or is it built on sand? Is it a boon to humanity, or a menace? It is thus a matter of principles more than of specific incidents and histories.

The religious connotation of the U.N. is apparent in most discussions thereof. Its opponents attack it as anti-Christian and anti-American, and, with no small heat, the proponents of the U.N. defend it as man's great hope for peace and true social order and see its critics as wicked, hate-filled heretics whom they denounce with conspicuous heat and hate.[1] It would be the course of wisdom for both sides to recognize that there is no lack of intelligence on both sides, and to concede the earnest faith of both parties, by recognizing that what divides them is not a matter of stupidity and "mental illness" but sharply contrasted articles of faith.

The U.N. thus must be seen in the context of its religious presuppositions. It is, historically, an outgrowth of Enlightenment concepts and of the religion of humanity.[2]

---

[1] See Gordon H. Hall: *The Hate Campaign Against the U.N., One World Under Attack.* Boston: Beacon Press, 1952.

[2] See R. J. Rushdoony, *This Independent Republic.* Nutley, N. J.: Craig Press, 1964.

First of all, the U.N. holds as its basic premise a thesis which has a long history in both religion and in politics, the doctrine of *salvation by law*. It believes that world peace can be attained through world law.[3] In Article I, Section 2 of Chapter I, "Purposes and Principles" of the Charter of the United Nations, it is declared that the purpose is

> To develop friendly relations among nations based on respect for the principle of equal rights and self-determination of peoples, and to take other appropriate measures to strengthen universal peace.[4]

The Charter makes clear that this purpose, while central, is not the only one. It has, however, received central attention from many proponents. Thus, Eichelberger held in 1955 that "The purpose of the United Nations is the maintenance of peace."[5] The problem of the U.N., he held, is political, i.e., methodological, for "The nations can agree upon a fool-proof system of disarmament if a political agreement or series of political agreements clears the way."[6] "Universal enforceable disarmament with collective security is the final answer to the threat of atomic destruction."[7] In other words, remove by force an aspect of man's environment, atomic weapons, and peace will follow. The U.N. needs to be strengthened to this end, he held. "The United Nations is in the shadowy area between an organization of states and a world government."[8] In 1960, Eichelberger re-affirmed his stand: "The purpose of the United Nations is to prevent war."[9] Its purpose, moreover, is to establish an international society for this purpose:

> The fundamental question could be stated in another way: is the United Nations the foundation of international

[3] See Grenville Clark and Louis B. Sohn: *World Peace Through World Law*. Cambridge: Harvard, 1958.
[4] For a commentary on this, see Hans Kelsen: *The Law of the United Nations*, A Critical Analysis of its Fundamental Problems, pp. 27 ff. New York: Praeger, 1950.
[5] Clark M. Eichelberger: *U.N.: The First Ten Years*, p. 8. New York: Harper, 1955.
[6] *Ibid.*, p. 51.
[7] *Ibid.*, p. 52.
[8] *Ibid.*, p. 89.
[9] Clark M. Eichelberger: *U.N.: The First Fifteen Years*, p. 8: cf. p. 4.

policy or an instrument which nations can use or reject as short-sighted self-interest dictates?

An examination of the Charter's Preamble, purposes and principles leads to the inescapable conclusion that the framers of the United Nations contemplated a dynamic international society. The world was at war. The peoples of many nations were serving together and making terrible sacrifices to win the war. They believed that with peace would come an international society strong enough to prevent war and build a just international order. The Atlantic Charter expressed this belief.[10]

The responsibilities of this international society must be "Planet Earth as a whole. And Planet Earth must be a moral and legal entity."[11]

This first premise, salvation by law, is a venerable one, with extensive religious support. It is, clearly, the basic doctrine of Judaism, and it is extensively present in traditional Christianity as in Thomism and Arminianism. It is the dominant doctrine of modernistic, social gospel Protestantism. Two aspects of this premise have already become manifest: First, that the hope and salvation of man and of society is through world law, and, second, that the essence or at least the primary factor in peace is environmental rather than personal. The environment must be altered by the removal of atomic weapons and by the addition of enforceable world law. This is a faith which many hold who are politically and economically conservative, as witness Senator Barry M. Goldwater, who holds that the U.N. needs re-direction, not abolition. The same is true of Felix Morley.[12] This position, however, cannot be consistently held by one who is a conservative or orthodox Christian because of its radical conflict with basic biblical doctrine. For the orthodox Christian, the law cannot save; it can only condemn. The law cannot create true peace and order; it cannot save man and society from the consequences of their sins. Christ alone is the prince and principle

---

[10] *Ibid.*, p. 125.

[11] *Ibid.*, p. 147.

[12] Barry M. Goldwater: *Why Not Victory?* p. 99 f. New York: Macfadden, 1962. Felix Morley wrote, "On the whole, the Charter is workmanlike and will be workable, if resolute popular will to that end is manifest in this and other countries": *The Charter of the United Nations, An Analysis*, p. 55. New York: American Enterprise Association, January, 1946.

of peace and of order, man's only savior and mediator. Neither introduction of law nor the removal of a part of man's environment are basic to the problem of peace, but rather regeneration through the saving work of Christ, His vicarious sacrifice, and sanctification in and through Him. Wars are not environmental in sources and origin but human. "From whence come wars and fightings among you? Come they not hence, even of your lusts that war in your members?" (James 4:1). Thus war is caused by sin, not by environment. Moreover, not all who are involved in war are equally sinners. Some are unjustly attacked and must defend themselves, so that peace as such is not always a virtue and can be as evil as any war. More accurately, war in itself cannot be called evil, for sin resides in man himself rather than in things, so that to seek the abolition of war is to evade the basic issue, the sin of man. And man's need is regeneration, which is not the function of the state. For the state to presume to save man is for the state to assume the prerogatives of the church. The Preamble to the Charter of the United Nations declares in part, "We the peoples of the United Nations determined to save succeeding generations from the scourge of war . . . to unite our strength to maintain international peace and security, and to ensure, by the acceptance of principles and the institution of methods, that armed force shall not be used, save in the common interest . . . have resolved to combine our efforts to accomplish these aims." The U.N. is thus "determined to save"; it is thus possessed with all the sense of inevitability and missionary fervor that any religious group possesses. It deserves to be regarded as a crusading missionary organization and to be respected for its idealistic faith, but, at the same time, regarded by orthodox Christians as a false and deadly faith, all the more deceptive because its idealism is premised on an anti-Christian faith. Inescapably, the hostility between the U.N., with its doctrine of the salvation of man and society by law, and orthodox Christianity is no less intense and bitter now than when the Sanhedrin felt that the future of the people and of their Temple required the death of Jesus (John 11:49-52).

A second basic premise of the U.N. is closely related to the first. Believing as it does in world peace through world law, it assumes that this world rule of law is necessarily the rule of morality. This illusion has been clearly expressed by Dean Roscoe Pound: "The real foe of absolution is law."[13] Yet the "courts are creatures of the political community," one advocate of this position affirms.[14] Is absolutism then really the enemy of law? Is not all positivistic law dedicated to absolutism? If no higher law is recognized, and if law is what man says it is, is not either the law or man absolutized, and, in either case, the controlling powers invested with total power? John Foster Dulles, in championing the U.N., clearly affirmed this same equation of "agreed law" and morality:

> It is generally agreed that a stable world order depends most of all upon the existence of an adequate body of international law which can be administered so as to secure justice. There is no such body of law today. Without it certain other steps cannot be taken. It is not safe to give coercive power to the Security Council or to any other international body unless that body is bound to administer agreed law. Without law, power is despotism. We ought not to try to impose international despotism upon others; neither should we consent to have it imposed upon ourselves.[15]

But the U.S.S.R. is both a despotism and has an agreed law. It is moreover democratic in structure. According to the Chairman of the U.S.S.R. Supreme Court:

> In the USSR justice is administered only by the courts, and all citizens are equal before the law and the court., irrespective of social or property status, office, nationality, race or religion.

> All courts in the USSR are elective. Every citizen of the USSR who enjoys the right of suffrage is eligible for election as judge or people's assessor. There is no

---

[13] Roscoe Pound: *Justice According to Law*, pp. 87-91; New Haven: Yale, 1951, cited in Victor G. Rosenblum: *Law as a Political Instrument*, p. 81; New York: Random House, 1962.

[14] Rosenblum, *idem*. Raymond Swing equated the U.N. developed into world government, as *law* and national sovereignty as lawlessness and *anarchy*, Raymond Swing: *In the Name of Sanity*, p. 116; New York: Harper, 1946.

[15] John Foster Dulles: *War or Peace*, p. 198. New York: Macmillan, 1950. On Dulles, see James J. Martin: *Meditations Upon the Early Wisdom of John Foster Dulles;* Mercer Island, Washington, 1958.

property or other qualification; all that is required is that the candidate shall have attained the age of 25.[16]

The Soviet Constitution affirms the rule of law, of Soviet law, from whence comes all true power and law. As Article 3 affirms, "All power in the U.S.S.R. belongs to the working people of town and country as represented by the Soviets of Working People's Deputies."[17]   Why not then accept the U.S.S.R. as an area of freedom, because ruled by law, rather than a depotism?   And yet even Socialists have been ready to apply such terms as "lynch procedure" to Soviet law.[18] What would constitute "agreed law" for Dulles?   Soviet scholars believe their society to be more truly concerned with the individual and with true humanism than "anti-humanist . . . monopoly capitalism."[19]   Dulles, as an earnest and even sanctimonious champion of modernist Christianity, had much to say about the righteous foundations of peace.[20]   Dulles defined the basis of law:

> Fundamentally, world peace depends upon world law, and world law depends upon a consensus of world opinion as to what is right and what is just. If there is wide disagreement about what is right and just, there will always be risk of war. Human nature is such that men always have believed—and I trust always will believe— as President Wilson put it in his war message to Congress, "The right is more precious than peace."

[16] Alexander Gorkin, "Guilty or Not Guilty—Who Decides?" in *USSR Soviet Life Today*, p. 37, December, 1963.

[17] Robert Le Fevre: *Constitutional Government Today in Soviet Russia*, The Constitution of the U.S.S.R. Annotated and explained, p. 19. New York: Exposition, 1962.

[18] Julius Jacobson, "Russian Law Enters the 'Final Stages of Communism'—1," in *New Politics*, p. 19-42, Fall, 1963, vol. II, no. 4.

[19] See Y. A. Zamoshkin, "Bureaucracy and the Individual," *The Soviet Review*, August, 1961, vol. 2, no. 8, pp. 20-38 and Nikolai Gei and Vladimir Piskunov, "Abstract Humanism and Socialist Humanism," *The Soviet Review*, June, 1961, vol. 2, no. 6, pp. 39-55.

[20] See John Foster Dulles, "The American People Need Now to be Imbued with a Righteous Faith," in Dulles, etc.: *A Righteous Faith for a Just and Durable Peace*, pp. 5-11. New York: Commission to Study the Bases of a Just and Durable Peace, Federal Council of Churches, 1942. For Dulles' piety, see Margaret Dulles Edwards, "Tomorrow's Legacy," *Bible Society Record*, vol. 109, no. 1 January, 1964, p. 12 f.

Experience in the United Nations shows that there is considerable agreement about what is right. That is particularly true between those who are influenced by one or another of the great religions. All the great religions reflect to some degree the moral or natural law, and that makes it possible to find many common denominators of right and wrong.

The great difficulty today is that the Communist rulers, who control so much of the world, are animated by an atheistic creed which denies the existence of a moral law or a natural law. To them, laws do not reflect justice, but are ways whereby those in power win their class war. For their beliefs and ours, it is impossible to find a common denominator. They do, however, pay attention to other people's sense of right and justice, because that affects what they will do and how they will act in any given situation. That is always of interest, even to despots.[21]

Three points are here apparent. First, Dulles, holding that "world peace depends upon world law," grounds that world law on no more than "a consensus of world opinion as to what is right and what is just." This consensus includes what the great religions have to say, and, if there be "wide disagreement," then "there will always be a risk of war." Dulles' foundation is thus purely immanent, a consensus or general will, and, because agreement is so important, it is logical to urge the world religions to suppress their differences, or at the least to make them unessential to their position. Second, Dulles made the very questionable assumption that all "great religions" are extensively agreed "about what is right." Orthodox Christianity would not accept this assumption. Third, Dulles held that, because Communism is atheistic, "it is impossible to find a common denominator" with respect to "a moral law or a natural law." One would logically assume that Dulles felt that the Communist states and all atheistic states have no place in the U.N. This, however, was not the case. In fact, Dulles in 1950 called for the recognition of Red China as a necessity if that government retained power "over a reasonable period of time."[22] How was this rationalized, when no *moral* common

---

[21] Dulles: *War or Peace*, p. 187.
[22] *Ibid.*, p. 190.

denominator exists, according to Dulles?   There is another common denominator, *power:*

> At the present stage of world development we should try to evolve a world organization that will form moral judgments and reflect as adequately as possible the quantity, quality, and intensity of power which will back these judgments.
> . . . Some persons would like to throw out Soviet Russia because we disagree with their representatives and they with us.   A world organization without Soviet Communists would be a much more pleasant organization. But they have power in the world, and if the United Nations gets away from that reality it becomes artificial and exerts less influence.   The United Nations should mirror more accurately, not less accurately, the reality of what is.[23]

The world must be saved by law, and law reflects power rather than morality.   Indeed, the United Nations must be beyond good and evil:

> I have now come to believe that the United Nations will best serve the cause of peace if its Assembly is representative of what the world actually is, and not merely representative of the parts which we like.   Therefore, we ought to be willing that all the nations should be members without attempting to appraise closely those which are "good" and those which are "bad."   Already that distinction is obliterated by the present membership of the United Nations.[24]

How can Dulles affirm the primacy of world law based "upon what is right and just" and then deny the validity, in that world order, of any appraisal of "good" and "bad" nations? The answer may lie in his central moral conviction:

> Our greatest need is to regain confidence in our spiritual heritage.   Religious belief in the moral nature and possibilities of man is, and must be, relevant to every kind of society, throughout the ages past and those to come.   It is relevant to the complex conditions of modern society.   We need to see that, if we are to combat

---

[23] *Ibid.*, p. 188.

[24] *Ibid.*, p. 190. Alexander Dallin concurs with this opinion in *The Soviet Union at the United Nations*, An Inquiry into Soviet Motives and Objectives, p. 212 f.; New York: Praeger, p. 213.   Soviet hopes from the U.N. are cited by Dallin, p. 192.

successfully the methods and practices of a materialistic belief.[25]

Orthodox Christianity affirms as the "greatest need," intellectually, the true recognition of the nature of Christ and of his saving power. The religion of humanity, which Dulles affirmed, found the nature of Christ irrelevant or at best a peripheral issue to "religious belief in the moral nature and possibilities of man." But for orthodox Christianity, man is a sinner, not the object of faith. Dulles felt it was a triumph of the U.N. that religious differences are regarded as irrelevant: "They mingle together on a basis of social and intellectual equality, irrespective of nation, race, sex, or creed." This, he held, was "genuine fellowship," practiced at the U.N. "more than anywhere else."[26] But for an orthodox Christian, who denies the equality of all creeds, this fellowship is anathema. All of these assumptions by the U.N., Dulles, and others, adds up to a simple equation: *the rule of law is the rule of morality, which is faith in man.* And this, in its own way, is a faith which Marxism emphatically holds. The world problem again appears, in this focus, *not as a need for regeneration but for re-organization, not a change in man's nature but a change in man's legal and insti-*

---

[25] *Ibid.,* p. 261.

[26] *Ibid.,* p. 65. While talking of equality, the U.N. is the most elitist of organizations. The General Assembly has no power but can only recommend action. The Security Council is vested with the actual power, while the Court executes its legal will. The Security Council can order against any country such measures as it deems including war, or total blockade, or "complete or partial interruption of economic relations, and of rail, sea, air, postal, telegraphic, radio and other means of communication" *Charter,* chapt. VII, articles 41, 42.

Dulles affirmed his belief in man. It is well to remember who the politicians are who have most often spoken of the need for such faith. Thus, it was Senator John C. Spooner, who, at the beginning of the 20th century, defended himself and other corrupt politicians, saying, "There is no treason in the Senate! The one man I despise most is he who takes upon his lips in blasphemy the good character of a woman; next to that is the man who will tear down the character of the man in public life. Above all things, my brothers, believe in your republic and in the general fidelity of your public servants." Faith in man is the constant plea of corrupt men. David Graham Phillips: *The Treason of the Senate,* p. 51. Stanford: Academic Reprints (1906 in original *Cosmopolitan* publication).

tutional environment. And this, of course was the Enlightenment hope.[27]

The goal of the U.N. is thus a humanistic order rather than a moral order in the sense of a transcendental law and the categories of good and evil. Humanism itself is equated with morality, and no other category can have any relevance. The Preamble makes clear that its allegiance is to "fundamental human rights," not to fundamental moral or religious rights or principles. The charter in stating its "Purposes and Principles," speaks clearly and plainly on this matter, affirming as a purpose and principle of the U.N.

> To achieve international cooperation in solving international problems of an economic, social, cultural, or humanitarian character, and in promoting and encouraging respect for human rights and for fundamental freedoms for all without distinction as to race, sex, language, or religion.[28]

It is moreover stated that "The Organization is based on the principle of the sovereign equality of all Members."[29] This is at least an unrealistic statement in view of the veto power granted to certain members. Again it is stated that the United Nations shall promote:

a. higher standards of living, full employment, and conditions of economic and social progress and development;
b. solutions of international economic, social, health, and related problems; and international cultural and educational cooperation; and
c. universal respect for, and observance of, human rights and fundamental freedoms for all without distinction as to race, sex, language, or religion.[30]

A third premise of the U.N. is thus clearly in view: it is a humanistic order, equalitarian and socialistic as well as totalitarian. It is denied that economics or religion are separate law spheres; both are subordinate to politics, to world politics, which must govern to secure "conditions of

---

[27] See Louis I. Bredvold: *The Brave New World of the Enlightenment.* Ann Arbor: University of Michigan Press, 1961.
[28] *Charter of the United Nations.* Chapt. I, Article 1, Sect. 3.
[29] *Charter,* I, 2, 1.
[30] *Charter* IX, 55.

economic and social progress and development." Religious differences are denied any validity, for no distinction as to religion is permitted. Not the freedom of economic law and religious activity but world legislation with respect to both is in view. Here is a position radically at odds with historic, orthodox Christianity. It is at odds also with the constitutional heritage of the United States. It is in power today, however, in both the U.N. and the United States. William O. Douglas, a U.S. Supreme Court Justice, has declared, "We believe that the extinction of any civilization, culture, religion, or life-ways is a loss to all humanity."[31] This of course immediately renders guilty every universal religion, i.e., every faith which believes that it is the hope of every man's salvation, because every such faith seeks to destroy by conversion every false faith. It renders guilty every American who longs for and works for the destruction of Communism. It is a demand for total tolerance because of total acceptance. Faith is in humanity as such, not in a transcendental moral and spiritual order. It is not "In God We Trust," but "In Man We Trust." According to Douglas, "As Mr. Justice Holmes once said, 'Universal distrust creates universal incompetence.' "[32] The biblical mandate, "Cease ye from man, whose breath is in his nostrils: for wherein is he to be accounted of?" (Isa. 2:22) and " . . . beware of men" (Matt. 10:17), is set aside, not on any empirical grounds of evidence, but on religious grounds. This strange new doctrine we are now told is the truly Christian and the truly American doctrine! Harry Dexter White, in his testimony before the House Un-American Activities Committee on August 13, 1948, affirmed this faith and said, in part, "My creed is the American creed . . . I am opposed to discrimination in any form, whether on grounds of race, color, religious, political belief, or economic status."[33] According to this

---

[31] William O. Douglas: *Democracy's Manifesto*, p. 44. Garden City, New York: Doubleday, 1962.

[32] *Ibid.*, p. 28.

[33] Nathan I. White: *Harry Dexter White, Loyal American,* p. 11 f.; cf. 22 f.; 41 f. published by Bessie (White) Bloom, Waban, Mass., 1956. White's "creed" is becoming U.S. Supreme Court law. Thus, in 1952, (343 U.S. 250) in *Beauharnais v. Illinois*, the Court "sanctioned state antihate legislation which imposed criminal sanctions on persons guilty of publishing statements which exposed the citizens of any race color,

position, there can logically be no discrimination against religious polygamy or cannibalism, or against communism. V. Frank Coe, on the stand on May 15, 1956, objected to being questioned as to his alleged Communist allegiance during a stated period, stating "that he should not be questioned about his political beliefs."[34] The logic of this is that there can be no challenge to what the humanistic world powers declare to be the status quo. As Lenny Bruce has stated it, "The religious leaders are 'what *should* be' . . . Let me tell you the truth. The truth is 'what is.' If 'what is' is, you have to sleep eight, ten hours a day, that is the truth. A lie will be: People need no sleep at all. Truth is 'what is.' "[35] Everything that exists, perversions, murders, and the like stands at least on an equality with good character as truth. Whatever this humanistic world order therefore declares to be "what is" is therefore "the truth." But it is a violation of orthodox Christian faith to see the state as the order of truth, which the Charter of the U.N. makes it to be. We need not go to the Universal Declaration of Human Rights, in which Mrs. Franklin D. Roosevelt had a major part, to substantiate this. The Charter itself makes clear that this universal equalitarianism is the true faith for all mankind. It is, moreover, *an absolute order, binding on all mankind.* "In the United Nations, as 'in my Father's house,' there 'are many mansions.'"[36] What does this mean? The Charter is explicit, as Cohen points out:

------

creed, or religion to contempt, derision, or obloquy." Paul G. Kauper: *Civil Liberties and the Constitution,* p. 58; Ann Arbor, Michigan: University of Michigan Press, 1962. Subsequently, the Illinois FEPC ruled that the Motorola Co. stop using ability tests for job applicants on the ground that the test was discriminatory and unfair in failing to make allowance for "culturally deprived and disadvantaged groups" and for "inequalities and differences in environment." See *Human Events,* vol. XXIV, no. 14, April 4, 1964, pp. 4, 13. In other words, the incompetent must be made privileged, and the competent penalized, to equalize men in the name of democracy.

[34] *Ibid.,* p. 408.

[35] Lenny Bruce, "How to talk dirty and influence people," *Playboy,* vol. 11 no. 1 January 1964, p. 182.

[36] Benjamin V. Cohen: *The United Nations, Constitutional Developments, Growths, and Possibilities,* p. 101.   The Oliver Wendell Holmes Lectures, 1961. Cambridge: Harvard, 1961.

The Charter of the United Nations is a treaty, but not an ordinary treaty. The Member States which subscribe to the Charter not only commit themselves to act in pursuance of the purposes and in conformity with the principles of the Charter, but authorize the Organization to ensure that non-Member as well as Member States act in accordance with the principles of the Charter, so far as may be necessary for the maintenance of international peace and security. The Charter looks toward, if it does not establish, a world-wide community of nations dedicated to the purposes and principles of the Charter.[37]

Lest it be assumed that this is merely Cohen's personal opinion, let us examine the Charter at this point:

The Organization shall ensure that states which are not Members of the United Nations act in accordance with these Principles so far as may be necessary for the maintenance of international peace and security.[38]

As a result, any act or agency of the U.N. which that body declares to be in accordance with its principles, such as UNESCO or the Universal Declaration of Human Rights (adopted near midnight, December 10, 1948, when the General Assembly met in Paris), is enforceable by armed force on any member or non-member state. That the U.N. intends to exert such force whenever and wherever it is able to do so can be safely assumed. In the meantime, certainly the constituent states are not lacking in politicians who are dedicated to "peaceful coexistence" as "a first step" towards "a staging area from which further advances toward the ideal global order can be launched."[39] To gain this peaceful coexistence, "The building of greater confidence and trust thus becomes a first objective of peaceful coexistence."[40] Again, faith in man is a basic perspective. Certainly the U.S. has dedicated itself to an attempt, no less zealously than the U.S.S.R., to create a world order and world peace.

---

[37] *Ibid.*, p. 2 f.

[38] *Charter*, I, 6. See also Eichelberger: *U.N.: The First Fifteen Years*, pp. 106-8; Kelsen, p. 75 f.

[39] Arthur N. Holcombe, chairman: *Peaceful Coexistence, A New Challenge to the United Nations*, p. 37. Twelfth Report, Commission to Study the Organization of Peace, Research Affiliate of the American Association for the United Nations New York: 1960.

[40] *Ibid.*, p. 19.

This is in evidence in the State Department, as in the U.N., and also in NATO, which is defined as "not merely a military alliance . . . it equally envisages permanent common action in the political and economic fields."[41]

These human rights which are to be imposed on all societies are basically hostile to every society. There is no country without a religious and racial orientation. In the U.S.S.R., the old Christian faith maintains its vitality underground. Each Soviet Republic is outwardly governed by men of its own racial origin. Thus, "in the Lithuanian Republic 90.6% of the judges are Lithuanians, and in the Armenian SSR 95% are Armenian."[42] Indeed, charges of anti-Semitism are levelled against the U.S.S.R., Jacobson charging that a high percentage of criminal executions involve Jews.[43] Others, like Bishop James A. Pike, have stated the reverse, namely, that the "Russians extend the melting pot idea to the point of persecution. In Russia, they say one can't be different. They say, 'We won't allow you to have cultural and religious separateness.'"[44] Whether either position is accurate is at least a matter of debate and probably questionable. Nonetheless, it can be safely said that it is likely that some race or races are the object of prejudice and discrimination in the U.S.S.R., and all historic religions as well. Certainly India discriminates against races and faiths alien to itself, as does Israel, Yemen, Ghana, and viritually every state in existence. Each properly represents the order of a particular people and a general or specific faith. The U.N. Charter gives grounds for the interference of that body into every national and religious state in existence in the name of total equality.

---

[41] North Atlantic Treaty Organization Information Service: *The North Atlantic Treaty Organization*, p. 7 f.; cf. p. 52. The NATO Handbook. Paris, 1962. See also John Fischer: *Master Plan U.S.A., An Informal Report on America's Foreign Policy and the Men Who Make It;* New York: Harper, 1951; Nelson A. Rockefeller: *The Future of Federalism*, New York: Atheneum, 1963; see the Department of State *Foreign Policy Briefs* for numerous instances; see President Lyndon B. Johnson's State of Union Message of January 8, 1964, *S. F. Examiner*, Thursday, January 9, 1964 p. 14

[42] Gorkin, *idem.*

[43] Jacobson, p. 34 ff.

[44] S. F. *Examiner*, Tuesday, January 7, 1964, p. 9.

The U.N. position, ostensibly anti-racist, is no less racist than the most fervent champions of race in history. Indeed, the liberal, religion of humanity, faith is simply a form of racism. There are two kinds of racism today. For the first, to belong to a particular race, white or black, Jewish or Arab, is all-important. Membership in a particular group is itself the mark of distinction and discrimination, and constitutes the dividing line. For the second form of racism, to belong to the human race is all-important. For both positions, *racial membership is the test, the ticket of admission and the guarantee of status.* Against this expanded or liberal form of racism, as against all forms of racism, orthodox Christianity enters a dissent. For the Christian, *character,* born of *faith,* is the test of man, not a particular race or the human race. Racial differences are recognized as real and as God-given, but the determinative fact concerning man is his relationship to God, not his fact of humanity. This is the biblical position; it is also the position which makes for progress by emphasizing *quality.* Quality is sought out and emulated. A people, discriminated against at one time, by emulation advance themselves, as witness the Irish in America. Therefore, in no uncertain terms, the orthodox Christian must regard the universal racism of the U.N. as a menace, destructive of the faith and detrimental to man.

The humanism of the U.N., as has been already indicated, rests on a religious doctrine of man, the fourth premise of its position. Because man must be trusted, and, because humanity as such is its standard apart from all distinctions of race or creed, idealism is held to be workable. All men, insofar as they are divorced from the alienating faiths of nationalism and supernatural religion, are assumed to seek peace and to desire it. Man is good, except when perverted by limited allegiances of country and faith. But idealism is one of the worst enemies of orthodox Christianity, in that it denies the doctrine of original sin and asserts that man's works and law can overcome the effects of sin and sin itself. It assumes that men's motives are good: they seek peace and progress when not perverted by *outside* influences. But orthodox Christianity says that men seek rather death and destruction apart from Christ. "All they that hate me love death" (Prov. 8:36). The idealism of unregenerate man is self-defeating and self-deceiving.

But the presupposition that man can save himself and his society by his own works and law rests not only on the assumption that man's basic problems are environmental rather than ethical and religious, i.e., due to a fallen nature, but also on the assumption that all human differences are of degree only, and not of kind. Hence they can be remedied or reconciled by man. Man must therefore seek relief, not from God but from himself magnified into the form of a world state. Orthodox Christianity, by its insistence on the sovereignty of God in salvation as in all things, cannot give assent to this faith.

But, in this perspective of the religion of humanity as incarnated in the U.N., the human problem is one of proper management and direction rather than a change of nature. What man needs thus is not the divine act but human engineering and planning.

By its failure to reckon with the fact of sin as the reality of human nature rather than an accident of environment and training, the U.N. is not only incompetent to deal with sin but especially prone to it. No legislative body is immune from the fact of sin. Every kind of institution, civil, religious, educational or otherwise, with any history of any length, has been characterized at some time or other, sometimes and often chronically, by corrupt practices, including graft and bribery. But in those bodies where a strong and active Christian faith prevails, that faith conditions and governs the limits of corruption, although it does not expect perfection this side of heaven. In the U.N., lacking in Christian faith and subscribing to an idealistic humanism, there is no such limitation. The voting is almost strictly in terms of the most corrupt kind of power politics and bribery.[45]

By failing to reckon with the fact of sin, the U.N. falls into the same fallacy as Marxism, that of seeing the backward peoples not simply as backward because of false faith and bad character but as *victimized*. The consequences of this position are favoritism for the backward and the delinquent

<hr>

[45] For one instance, see Alfred Lilienthal: *What Price Israel?*, pp. 61 ff., with reference to Palestine; Chicago: Regnery, 1953. This, however, is merely one case among many.

(as well as the criminal), and the penalizing of the advanced. "Burden-sharing" is imposed on the advanced in the form of extensive grants in aid to other nations.[46] These nations are not termed backward or degenerate but rather "the less developed members."[47] Progress is seen as an accident of environment and opportunity, not as a consequence of religious character.

It is possible to cite at length the political consequences of the false premises of the U.N. A few will suffice. The Charter provides for centralization of power and vastly expands the powers of state. Its officials are appointed. Property rights and trial by jury are omitted from the Charter. The U.S. Constitution, on the other hand, both separates and limits the powers and the branches of the federal government. It provides for elected officials, protects property rights, and protects the right of trial by jury. The Constitution denies to the federal union any jurisdiction over religion; the Charter forbids all religious distinctions, *which is tantamount to abolishing all religions save the religion of humanity.* Established to keep the peace, it has failed to keep the peace.[48] While talking much of human rights, as in The Covenant on Human Rights, its "every statement of right places in government hands unlimited authority to define the right and to restrict every exercise of it."[49] It has been consistently a threat to historic liberties.[50] The U.N. has been characterized in its brief history by one sorry scandal after another, and one failure after another: the Bang-Jensen case, Hungary, Tibet, Palestine, Goa, the Congo, Angola, and many, many more.[51]

---

[46] See Pierre Uri: *Partnership for Progress, A Program for Transatlantic Action,* p. 45. Published for the Atlantic Institute by Harper and Row, New York, 1963.

[47] Eichelberger: *The U.N.: The First Fifteen Years,* p. 130 f.

[48] See "There is No Peace—18 Years 57 Wars," *The Indianapolis News,* Monday, April 29, 1963.

[49] V. Orval Watts: *Should We Strengthen the United Nations?* p. 29, Colorado Springs: The Freedom School, 1961.

[50] Alice Widener: *Behind the U.N. Front.* New York: Bookmailer, 1962. Widener has an interesting chapter on the U.N. advocate, Clark M. Eichelberger pp. 87-94.

[51] See U.S. Senate Committee on the Judiciary: *The Bang-Jensen Case,* Washington: Government Printing Office, 1961; Julius Epstein: "The Bang-Jensen Tragedy," *American Opinion,* vol. III, no. 5, May,

The U.N. believes in salvation by law, but in no historic sense does it have law. The two central definitions of law are (1) the binding custom or practice of a community, or (2) the commandments or revelations of God. The U.N. has no community of law, nor any revealed religious basis. As a result, its decisions, as well as those of the World Court, are bound to be an injustice to most men. Law, however, can also be the rule of conduct and action prescribed by a supreme governing authority and enforced thereby. Such law from early times has been called tyranny. The laws of the U.N. thus, however well-intentioned, and the decisions of the World Court, however much informed by a zeal for humanity, are inescapably a tyranny to most men. To impose the laws of Islam upon a Jain and a Christian is surely tyranny, even as would be the imposition of Jewish law upon a Moslem. Law can be as much an instrument of invasion and tyranny as can bayonets; alien laws strike at the heart of a culture and at its vitals. In the name of defending all cultures, the U.N. is a new humanistic culture aimed at destroying all others by means of the imperialism of world law and a world police. It is not surprising that the U.N. is unpopular with many, and this distaste for the U.N. is no doubt a factor among others in the financial delinquency

---

1960; *Congo July 1960 Evidence,* Statement by Mr. Merchiers, Belgian Minister of Justice; *46 Angry Men, The 46 Civilian Doctors of Elisabethville Denounce U.N.O. Violations in Katanga,* Belmont, Mass., 1962; *On the Morning of March 15,* Boston: Portuguese-American Committee on Foreign Affairs, n.d.; On the double role of Lt. General Vasiliev, with the U.N. and with the North Korean invasion, in the Korean War, see U.S. Department of Defense, Office of Public Information, release no. 465-54, Saturday, May 15, 1954; Michel Sturdza: *World Government and Internal Assassination,* Belmont, Mass., 1963, p. 18, cites Professor Hans Morgenthau of Chicago as stating that "The International Government of the United Nation, stripped of its legal trimmings, then, is really the International Government of the United States and the Soviet Union acting in unison;" the citation is from Hans J. Morgenthau, "The New United Nations, What It Can't and Can Do." *Commentary,* November 1958, vol. 26, no. 5, p. 376. Morgenthau, who favors the U.N., points out that the U.N.'s legal power is in the Security Council, which has "only two . . . really great powers," the U.S. and the U.S.S.R. When these two work in unison, they are the U.N.; "if they are disunited—there will be no international government at all." One can conclude, therefore, from the activities of the U. N. that there is a growing range of action in unison.

of many members with respect to dues. The U.S. is paying "nearly half of the U.N. peacekeeping operations," among other things.[52]

While weak in many areas, the U.N. is clearly strong in the support it gains from certain religious circles, especially where the religion of humanity is clearly in view. During World War I, the European World Conscience Society distributed to the clergy in the English-speaking world a book dedicated to affirming "the spiritual unity of man" as a scientific fact, "Proclaiming his social unity," and "preaching the gospel of political unity."[53] The oneness of all races, religions, and states was the new gospel of this agency.

During World War II, the joint operation of all religions to create the new world order was urged through a Federal Council of Chuches Commission. Everett R. Clinchy urged, "Let Protestants, Catholics and Jews and those of other religious faith live to prove that men can together build the natural world without and the intellectual and moral world within so that the united peoples of the world shall create a prosperity, as Lincoln suggested, whose course shall be forward and which as long as the earth endures shall never pass away."[54]

The National Council of Churches has repeatedly called for support of the U.N. In its 1963 Philadelphia Assembly message, after calling for "racial brotherhood and justice," the "National Council's Message to the Churches" went on to say, in terminology common to the religion of humanity:

> As churches, we must actively support the United Nations and adequate aid for developing nations; must press for significant steps toward disarmament and for diversion of enormous resources now devoted to the arms race to a frontal attack on the unmet needs of mankind;

[52] *Oakland (Calif.) Tribune*, "Showdown in the U.N." editorial, p. 23 Wednesday, January 8, 1964.

[53] Walter Walsh: *The World Rebuilt*, p. 27. London: Allen and Unwin, 1917.

[54] Everett R. Clinchy, "Christians Must Seek the Cooperation of Other Faiths " in Dulles, etc.: *A Righteous Faith*, p. 36. f. On the National Council, see *The Dan Smoot Report*, vol. 10, no. 2, January 13, 1964, "National Council of Churches."

and must recognize that revolutionary movements of our time may be new thrusts for human dignity and freedom.[55]

These general terms could serve to give dignity to *any* revolutionary movement, for which do not claim to seek "human dignity and freedom?"

On April 10, 1963, Pope John XXIII addressed an encyclical, "Pacem in Terris," to the Roman Catholic Church and "to all men of good will," calling for a world community without Christian faith as its premise.[56] Although some churchmen sought to give the encyclical a conservative perspective, others, like Father Joseph Walsh, C.S.P., saw in it radical directions:

> I personally never thought I would see the day when a Pope would talk about the human family having entered upon an advance towards limitless horizons—this, from the successor of a Pope who, a hundred years ago, was condemning liberalism with its claims of man's capacity to grow and perfect himself as somehow opposed to the innate limitations of humanity. This change is of great significance for the way in which Catholicism and Catholics in general will view the future and the problems of mankind. Man is now looked upon as capable of advancing towards limitless horizons. The Pope very much wants to immerse his institution in that advance.[57]

Some men have openly called for a world religion, or a United Religions order comparable to the United Nations. Thus, Dr. Luther H. Evans, Dartmouth College professor of political science and ex-director general of UNESCO has said, "The peace of the world demands not only the existence of the United Nations, but also a United Religions."[58]   But

---

[55] "National Council's Message to the Churches," *Presbyterian Life*, vol. 17, no. 1, January 1, 1964, p. 26.

[56] *The New York Times, Western Edition*, Thursday. April 11, 1963, pp. 1, 5-7, Arnoldo Cortesi, "Pope Urges Formulation of World Nation to Insure Peace and the Rights of man."

[57] "Pacem in Terris: an unexpected ally," interview with Father Joseph Walsh, in *new university thought*, Summer, 1963, vol. 3, no. 1, p. 17. For a contrary opinion of the encyclical, from a conservative, see Sister M. Margaret Patricia, "Justice Has Sprung From The Earth," 1963.

[58] Hector Pereyra-Suarez, "Blueprint for Religious Union," in *Liberty*, September-October, 1963, vol. 58, no. 5, p. 8.

"conflict, not peace will be the consequence of pressures for religious unity."[59]

The religious tension and conflict between orthodox Christianity and the religion of humanity, to mention no others, cannot be reconciled. Orthodox Christianity sees the problem of man as "a disruption between man and God. . . the troubles man has are due to a broken relationship with his Maker." The religion of humanity points instead "to the disruption within human personality. It is said that ideally man is a 'whole' person and that breakdowns in this wholeness cause the troubles man experiences." Here the *basic* problem is not "a disruption between man and God" but "the *basic* problem is rather a disruption within—and between man and man" requiring, among other things, the restoration of "the dimensions of brotherhood."[60] Dr. Franklin Littell has stated the aim of the faith is "the renewal of the social structure. . .not the saving of individual souls," for "God wants to restore responsibility to a rebellious and broken social order."[61]

This is a revolutionary, messianic, and anti-historical religious faith, for its goal is the end of history in the perfect social order. As one man has stated it, "The realm of childhood is, by nature, a real democracy. Children do not know the past; they live in the present; they have no anguish of the future."[62] Not only must all men and all religions be equal, but apparently all times and ages as well!

Certainly, this faith offers an easy equalization of all standards. When the Rev. Adam Clayton Powell, Negro Congressman and civil rights leader, was criticized for his moral conduct, his answer was forthright and rigorously honest. "I know what they're saying, 'You should be better than other people because you might embarrass the civil

---

[59] *Ibid.*, p. 11, the concluding comment of Hector Pereyra-Suarez.

[60] Editorial, "A Story of Two Sermons," *The Presbyterian Journal*, vol. XXII, no. 33, December 11, 1963, p. 10.

[61] G. Aiken Taylor, "A Theology for the NCC," *The Presbyterian Journal*, vol. XXII, no. 35, December 25, 1963, p. 8.

[62] Sigmund Livingston: *Must Men Hate?* p. 1. Cleveland: Crane Press, 1944, revised edition.

rights struggle.' Why should I be better than other people? Hell, man, I'm fighting for equality!"[63]

A one world order requires a one world religion in order to be undergirded by a living fabric of faith and law. The issue will be joined, accordingly, in the arena of Christian faith rather than in political action, for the dynamics of action are in the realm of faith. For the one world order to advance, it must wage war against religion, orthodox Christianity in particular. There is thus no escaping the fact of religious warfare. Those who refuse to offer incense to the new caesars will face both hostility and persecution. But even more certainly, they will have from their faith the assurance of victory (I John 5:4,5).

---

[63] Claude Lewis: *Adam Clayton Powell*, p. 124. New York: Gold Medal Books, 1963. Lewis a Negro and a *Newsweek* reporter, speaks of Powell as "a brilliant man who might have become a Messiah," p. 127. Lewis, lacking the consistency of thought which characterizes Powell, fails to recognize the logic and integrity of Powell's position, which one can surely dissent with, while recognizing its clarity of structure and thought.

CHAPTER VIII

THE CONSPIRACY VIEW OF HISTORY

In the eyes of most intellectuals, the hallmark of intellectual acceptability is to view history as the outworking of impersonal forces and factors, whereas the epitome of absurd, irrational and even dangerously reactionary thinking is to regard history as in any sense involving *conspiracy*. Such a view is primitive and naive; it is a form of belief in the devil, we are told. As one scholar summarizes this perspective,

> In the modern world, the Devil has all the characteristics of the medieval Devil, translated into modern terms. The Devil is ubiquitous, insidious, powerful, and morally corrosive. He must be identifiable and recognizable as an image, but unidentifiable when at work. Groups that can serve as Devil images must therefore be ubiquitous, insidious, powerful, morally corrosive; they must be identifiable as groups, but capable of disguise—indeed, of making themselves indivisible—in their operations. "The Russian people" or "The American People" can therefore not serve as Devil. They are geographically localized, and they are much like other people, once you come to know them. But Communism, Wall Street Capitalism, Imperialism, Freemasonry, and so on, meet the requirements.
>
> The operations of the fiend are worldwide and secret. There exists a World Conspiracy aiming at nothing less than the utter destruction of its foes, followed by world domination. The Communist World Conspiracy works through espionage, sabotage, and revolution, the Capitalist Conspiracy through incitement to war and through "spies, wreckers, and saboteurs." The Jewish Conspiracy according to Hitler works through race-mixing, cultural poisoning, and warmongering against the German *Volk*.

The Great Conspiracy has a secret Master Plan which may accidentally become known.[1]

It is best, at this point, to call attention to the common dictionary definitions, in the Merriam-Webster Dictionary, Second Edition, of conspiracy, which means (1) a "combination of men for an evil purpose; an agreement between two or more persons to commit a crime in concert, as treason; a plot"; (2) "Combination of men for a single end; a concurrence, or general tendency, as of circumstances, to one event; harmonious action"; (3) *"Law.* An agreement, manifesting itself in words or deeds, by which two or more persons confederate to do an unlawful act, or to use unlawful means to do an act which is lawful; confederacy." It is at once obvious that, in all three senses, conspiracy exists and that, in the second sense it is present in all kinds of organizations and institutions. Indeed, at least in this sense, university professors are continually involved in combinations of men working for a single end, with reference to their department and school, with reference to the trustees, and to the country at large. Moreover, these intellectuals would not deny that a Communist International exists whose goal is world communism, either through indoctrination, subversion, or revolution. They might approve or disapprove of that organization, but its existence is not denied. In justice to these critics of the conspiracy idea, it should be noted that for them the basic issue lies elsewhere. Even if there is a self-proclaimed world-wide Communist International in action, which is by its own profession a *conspiracy,* it can *only* be understood in terms of unconscious, *impersonal* historical forces. In this perspective, to see a conspiracy as a conspiracy is a naive mis-reading of history, a failure to analyze its basic currents, and an attempt to see historical froth as substance. To "expose" conspiracies is thus seen as *a confusion of appearance with reality* and an evasion of the basic problems and conflicts of history.

At this point, it becomes apparent, first, that many conservatives have failed to do the liberals justice because

---

[1] Gregor Sebba, "Symbol and Myth in Modern Rationalistic Societies," in Thomas J. J. Altizer, William A. Beardslee, J. Harvey Young: *Truth, Myth and Symbol,* p. 154 f. Englewood Cliffs, N. J.: Prentice-Hall, 1962.

they have failed to recognize the nature of the liberal position. Rather than an unwillingness to face the facts, the problem is a different framework for the facts and even a different concept of what constitutes a fact. For the conservative, the Communist conspiracy is a *fact;* for the liberal, the *fact* is rather deep-seated, and irrepressible historical forces which manifest themselves in various phenomena, and, not the phenomena, but the underlying forces are to be reckoned with. Between the two positions no real "dialogue" has existed, because there has been no recognition of the radically different concepts of factuality which undergird them. Second, it is further apparent that many conservatives, as witness the libertarians, are liberals in their concept of factuality. For the libertarians, factuality is impersonal; it is the inescapable outworking of economic forces and has no place for the conspiracy idea. The libertarian differs from the Marxist, not in his concept of factuality, but only in his interpretation as to what constitutes economic forces and laws. In either case, this position, while ostensibly the faith of humanism and a faith in man, is actually the surrender of man and of any integral humanism to a blind impersonalism. Man's government is surrendered to impersonal forces and factors, and the essence of true order is non-personal; history cannot be surrendered to the personal predilections of individuals.

The result of *impersonalism* is *the reign of totalism,* and a drift into totalitarianism. Impersonalism leads many economists of the classical school of liberalism to see the reign of impersonal economic law as operative despite all man may do. The psychologists sees man, similarly, under the power of impersonal psychological reflexes common to all men, either as unconditioned reflexes or as reflexes conditioned by particular forms of environmental stimuli. The meaning of man is thus primarily and essentially psychological. The biologist sees the impersonal facts of biology as determinative of all men. The physicist has a more basic interpretation and sees life and matter in terms of a determination by a theory of physical origins, and so on. Each area is thus an area of inevitable and total law, and other areas are to be seen, very often, in terms of the laws or concepts of the partisan's sphere. None see man as in any sense capable of transcending these *laws of origin,* because, man having been derived from these sources, according to their evolutionary presuppositions, is bound by his origins, which determine his nature. But, if we hold that man is a creature of God, not of "nature," and is created in the image of God, then man must be understood in terms of his origin, God. The law spheres of nature are created by God and are *under God,* and *under man in Christ.* Man's *laws of origin* are to be sought, not in "nature" which is *under* him, but in the word of God, which is *over* him and governs him. This word is the personal word of the triune God to man, His creature. There is thus relatively little argument with reference to predestination; the question is this, is the predestination natural or is it supernatural? Is the "eternal decree" governing man a totally immanent one, derived from natural forces, or is it a totally transcendental one, having its source in the sovereign God? The adherents of humanistic planning are champions of predestination also, of a coming or developing predestination. In their theory, a totally immanent predestination is necessary for man's salvation, and this immanent predestination is cradle to grave security, planning and control.

But orthodox Christianity insists on a transcendental predestination and refuses to place man under the determinism of nature. This is his area of creaturely kingship and power, of liberty, not of slavery. But impersonalism denies this. It is guilty of the reduction of all of life to impersonal natural operations and forces. And, since each law sphere, biology, psychology and the like, see man as under their law, they deny him both transcendence and liberty, and underrate other law spheres in the name of their determining law. Each area tends to claim total law for itself and to become totalitarian as it gains power.

This then, is the basic issue: Is factuality personal or impersonal? The liberal position has its variations. For Marx, economic forces are determinative; for Darwin, they are biological, for Freud, biological and psychological in terms of the basic biology of man. Some interpretations of this basically impersonal factuality can be, as we have noted, quite "conservative" with reference to a particular area of thought, but the common denominator of all is that all factuality is ultimately impersonal and is grounded in impersonal being. This impersonal being has evolved into various forms, and is characterized by a variety of developments, phenomena, and epiphenomena, of which consciousness and personality are instances. But the essence of being is impersonal, and the truth about factuality on which all valid knowledge must be premised is its basic and ultimate impersonality. History therefore must be read in terms of forces and movements which are impersonal, for to read it otherwise is to mistake accident for substance. There may be and are differences of opinion as to the determinative forces, but, for any intellectually respectable position, there can be no dissent as to their ultimate impersonality.

With this position, the orthodox Christian must dissent. As Cornelius Van Til has repeatedly pointed out, the Christian, believing in a completely self-conscious and personal God, believes that all created factuality is personal because it is the work of that personal God and derives its being and its interpretation from Him. There is no such thing as brute factuality, nor is there any impersonal factuality. The universe is not the product of blind, impersonal forces but the handiwork of the triune God. Instead of being interpreted in terms of impersonal, evolving factors, it must be interpreted in terms of the very personal purposes of a wholly personal God. To the extent that impersonalism enters into a philosophy which is ostensibly Christian, to that extent it is non-Christian and even anti-Christian. History moves, therefore, not in terms of impersonal forces but the very clearly personal decree of the ontological trinity. Because God is truly sovereign, history is not only to be read in terms of Christian personalism, but also recognized as under law, predestinated, deriving its creaturely liberty in the fact of the ultimate and undergirding government of God. In this perspective, economic, psychological and other factors are not denied, but they are not viewed as grounded in an impersonal reality and context but rather as aspects of a personal environment. Since man's true and ultimate environment is the personal and triune God, man's immediate environment cannot be impersonal factuality but is rather the world of God's creation, to which man is organically related by virtue of his creation in God's image and his calling to be prophet, priest and king under God over that world.

History, therefore, is not the outworking of impersonal forces but a personal conflict between the forces of God and anti-God, Christ and antichrist, with the ultimate victory assured to God and His Christ. The Bible as a whole presents a view of *history as conspiracy*, with Satan and man determined to assert their "right" to be gods, knowing, or determining, good and evil for themselves (Genesis 3:5). From beginning to end, this is the perspective of Scripture, and only a wilful misreading of it can lead to any other position.

In Psalm 2, this concept of history as conspiracy is briefly summarized. It should be noted that no other psalm is more frequently quoted in the New Testament; *Revelation* is in a sense an expansion of the same vision. Psalm 2 was written by David in terms of a personal and national event, and he saw the cosmic crisis behind the local affair. The whole world is seen as organized against the Lord in deliberate opposition to His rule, for David sees, not himself, but the Lord Messiah as the true king. In verses 1-3, the worldly conference of the conspiracy is depicted: "Why do the heathen (or nations) rage, and the people imagine a vain thing?" The nations rage against their bondage to God, and they take counsel or conspire against God and His Christ, planning to create their own world order and law in contempt of Him. In vv. 4-6, the heavenly confidence is revealed, and the certainty of the outcome. God laughs, He holds the nations in derision, but He gives evil time to mature, so that the issue becomes clear-cut. His Son is already the ordained king of creation. In vv. 7-9, the Messiah declares the divine decree in relation to Himself. His kingship is authorized as the Son of God, v. 7; God endows Him with all the earth, v. 8; He is given the power to overcome all His enemies, v. 9, and to destroy the conspiracy; to Him the peoples and realms are promised as a gift for His victory and kingship. In vv. 10-12, the nations are exhorted to abandon the conspiracy against God and His Christ or else face destruction. They must either accept the scepter of Christ's authority and blessing or be broken with the rod of iron. To this view of history, Jesus Christ gave His authority, declaring of the men of His day, as they conspired against Him, that their conspiratorial thesis was the seizure of the Kingdom and inheritance by the murder of the heir (Matt. 21:38). While the liberals may view belief in the conspiracy view of history as absurd, or even as a sign of membership in the "lunatic fringe," the orthodox Christian must assert it to be basic to the philosophy of history.

But simply to accept the view of history as conspiracy is not in itself an acceptance of the perspective of orthodox Christianity, for history is replete with conspiracies and conspiracies, many of which, while very important, serve only to deflect the minds of many from the central and essentially religious issues. To speak of the multiplicity of conspiracies is enough to make many liberals wince with embarrassment at the "shallowness" of such a consideration, but the issue needs to be faced with the recognition that intellectual respectability in the eyes of either the liberals or anyone else is an irrelevant matter in the discussion of any question. We must leave the dead to bury the dead.

First of all, as we have noted, the conspiracies at any given moment of history are many, and, the more crucial the issues, the more extensive the conspiracies. Let us examine briefly the administration of President Grant. Among the more prominent conspiracies were the Credit Mobilier affair, the gold conspiracy of Jim Fisk and Jay Gould,[2] and the Whiskey Ring. There was also the Union League conspiracy in the South, and the Radical Republican reconstruction plan,[3] the Ku Klux Klan, Loyal League, White Camelias, White Brotherhood and the Pale Faces, all secret societies.[4] Before the War, there was the Secret Six conspiracy with John Brown, as has been noted, and Benjamin

---

[2] Henry Adams, "The New York Gold Conspiracy," in *The Great Secession Winter of 1860-61 and Other Essays*, pp. 157-189. New York: Sagamore Press, 1958.

[3] Peter Joseph Hamilton: *The Reconstruction Period*, vol. XVI of Francis Newton Thorpe: *The History of North America*, Philadelphia: Barrie, 1905. E. Merton Coulter: *The South During Reconstruction, 1865-1877;* Baton Rouge: Louisiana State University Press, 1947. R. J. Rushdoony: *This Independent Republic*, chapt. 7.

[4] Hamilton, pp. 431-451. Myrta Lockett Avary: *Dixie After The War,* An Exposition of Social Conditions Existing in the South, During the Twelve Years Succeeding the Fall of Richmond, pp. 263-280; New York: Doubleday, Page, 1906.

Morgan Palmer's charge of a Jacobin program.[5] But all this is only to scratch the surface. These are either the minor or the unsuccessful conspiracies. Thus, the *known* conspiracies of the Grant administration, as of most eras, are often not the most important ones. The successful and continuing conspiracies of history are never admitted to be conspiracies. Their known activities are extolled as virtues and patriotic works, never as illicit activities. Legitimacy is the reward of success, and only that which is seemly is admitted as acceptable party history.

A second fact characterizes conspiracies, namely, that the conspiracy view of history is denied not only on philosophical premises but also on conspiratorial grounds. Thus, the existence of the Illuminati is either by-passed completely or else its life is held to have been brief and ineffectual, this in spite of the telling testimony of men like Abbe Barruel and John Robison. After the supposed suppression and death of that conspiracy, Rev. Jedidiah Morse discovered its existence in the United States and exposed it but could not bring about its suppression.[6] George Washington clearly accepted as true the facts stated by Morse.[7] Freemasonry, the Illuminati, and Unitarianism were extensively interlocking, and were the object of an extensive counter-movement in the early 19th century, but the very Anti-Masonic Party was so infiltrated that its presidential candidate was a secret Mason. The National Bank idea was seen as a part of this conspiracy.[8]

---

[5] For a wartime Confederate conspiracy, see James D. Horan: *Confederate Agent, A Discovery in History.* New York: Crown, (1954) 1960.

[6] Jedidiah Morse: *A Sermon, Exhibiting the Present Dangers, and Consequent Duties of the Citizens of the United States of America,* Charlestown, April 25, 1799; and *A Sermon, Delivered at the New North Church in Boston . . .,* May 7, 1798 Boston.

[7] Vernon Stauffer: *New England and the Bavarian Illuminati,* p. 342f. New York 1918. For a charge of conspiracy from that era, see Alexander Addison: *Rise and Progress of Revolution: A Charge to the Grand Juries of the County Courts of the Fifth Circuit of the State of Pennsylvania at December Sessions, 1800.* Philadelphia: Whitehall, 1801.

[8] Charles McCarthy: *The Antimasonic Party: A Study of Political Antimasonry in the United States, 1827-1840,* p. 397 f., cf. p. 396 for remarks of Seward: p. 557 f. See also Steven's resolution in Pennsylvania; p. 557 f., Annual Report, American Historical Association for

Esoteric Freemasonic writers have asserted the tie between Freemasonry and the Illuminati.[9]

We have seen, first, that there is generally a multiplicity of conspiracies, and, the more they succeed, the less they are recognized. Second, conspiracies are denied on conspiratorial grounds. Let us now consider a third aspect of the problem. The commonly admitted conspiracies are those of the opposition. The Communists see themselves as the necessary development of history and only their enemies as a reactionary conspiracy against history. The liberal establishment sees itself as intelligence and progress incarnate, not as a Fabian conspiracy. The conspiracy for them is on the right. The conservatives recognize Communist, Fabian and sometimes Zionist conspiracies, but will not admit that they are conspiring against them, for what they represent is a defense of our constitutional heritage. Each may or may not be right, but to be in the right does not nullify the fact of conspiracy.

Similarly, in the religious arena, the belief in conspiracy is prevalent. The Jews have their various organizations, including the Anti-Defamation League, to defend themselves against Christian majorities and "anti-Semitic" conspiracies,

---

1902, vol. I, pp. 365-574; Washington: Government Printing Office, 1903. In Sylvanus Cobb, Universalist and Mason, there is an interesting conjunction of various ideas under the banner of the Fatherhood of God and the Brotherhood of Man; *Autobiography of the First Forty-One Years of the Life of Sylvanus Cobb, to which is added a Memoir by Sylvanus Cobb, Jr.;* Boston: Universalist Publishing House, 1867. On the Illuminati and its refounding in Dresden in 1880, see Nesta H. Webster: *World Revolution, The Plot Against Civilization,* p. 235; London: Constable. 1921. During the American Revolution, Negro Freemasonry was organized, and Prince Hall, the Negro Mason, was in closer contact with the Grand Lodge of England than were white Masons then and for some time subsequently; Harry E. Davis: *A History of Freemasonry Among Negroes in America,* p. 18; United Supreme Council, Prince Hall Affiliation, 1946. The Negroes expected to be used by the British against the white colonials at the opportune moment, to be given power over them, David Hawke: *In the Midst of a Revolution,* p. 90; Philadelphia; University of Pennsylvania Press, 1961. Between these two facts the only known connection is that the British Masons favored the group most likely to be of use to the Empire. For the more general relationship of Freemasonary and revolution, see Bernard Fay; *Revolution and Freemasonary, 1680-1800;* Boston: Little, Brown, 1935.

[9] See Foster Bailey: *The Spirit of Masonry,* pp. 22 f., 26 f.; Tunbridge Wells, Kent: Lucis Press 1957, and his *Changing Esoteric*

but they will not refer to themselves as a conspiracy. The Roman Catholics wage a long-range struggle against the revolt of Jews and Protestants against the Catholic West, but they will not admit to any conspiracy on their part. Conspiracy is Protestant and Jewish in their eyes. Protestants are horrified at attempts of Roman Catholics to convert the United States to Roman Catholicism, and of Jews to maintain a dual citizenship and to eliminate the Christian framework of the country, but they will not recognize conspiracy except in the opposition. But conspiracies can be either good or bad, and this is well known. The reluctance to call one's own position a conspiracy rests on the premise that destiny cannot be conspiracy; it is historical inevitability. Only that which seeks to conspire against destiny is conspiracy, which is some kind of desperate, dangerous and yet futile attempt to stay the clock of history. And, in a very real sense, there is truth in this opinion. If there be any pattern, purpose or direction in history, all counter-movements will, historically, be regarded as conspiracies against that nature or destiny. On the other hand, only those who fully believe in a transcendental predestination can avoid conspiracy, for they alone can rest in the confidence that it will be God's work. In most instances, the conception of destiny involves a fair amount of human pattern and purpose identified as ultimate, and hence conspiracy.

But to represent destiny in any sense does not mean to represent either perfect virtue or infallibility. The Bible points clearly to the wretched nature of the chosen people of the Old Covenant, and the heresies and sins of the elect people of the

---

Values, 1954, which claims Col. House as a higher disciple, and Woodrow Wilson as a "sixth Ray disciple," p. 59; F. D. Roosevelt as a part of the operation the World Servers work, pp. 80-83; The Four Freedoms as "an Hierarchically inspired statement," p. 62; 1963 as a "great Hierarchial year" for the advancement of humanity. pp. 73-92, and world unity as a goal. On Masonry, see also E. Cahill: *Freemasonry and the Anti-Christian Movement;* Dublin Gill, 1930. Arthur Preuss: *A Dictionary of Secret and Other Societies*, St. Louis: Herder, 1924; and Preuss: *A Study in American Freemasonry*, second edition, St. Louis, Herder, 1908. See also *The Secret Warfare of Freemasonry Against Church and State* (no author given) London: Burns, Oates, 1875. In particular see Albert Pike: *Morals and Dogma of the Ancient and Accepted Scottish Rite of Freemasonry*, Southern Jurisdiction, U. S., 1915, Charleston A.M., 5641.

New Covenant. The various commanding empires of history, from Rome to the United States today, have not been preserved from grievous sins at their highest points. No party, religious group, or race, however confident of its cause and destiny, can afford the luxury of assuming that the righteousness of a cause a man affirms is identical with his own nature. The answer, on the other hand, is not mutual tolerance, for unity and brotherhood movements are either desertions of one's position for the religion of humanity, or else they are hypocrisy. The answer is not to be *one,* but to be *under law* rather than to claim to be *law incarnate.* It is the course of common sense to see one's real enemies as dangerous and evil, but it is also the course of wisdom to see oneself as also a sinner, different only to the extent that God's grace is operative in us.

A fourth consideration with respect to conspiracy makes evident, however, that history will see no lessening of the intensity of struggle and counter-movements, for, *the nearer to total war, the near to total conspiracy.* In the 18th Century, wars were fought, prior to the French Revolution, by small armies, usually professionals, with general respect for civilian life and property. General engagements were avoided, and a pressure of armed force and diplomacy was used on a limited scale to gain limited ends. Earlier, The Thirty Years War had been total war because total stakes were at issue. As The Thirty Years War began, the principals had certain basic and far-reaching issues at stake. Their total commitment made for the collapse of all law and order in terms of the greater eminence given to the cause, with the result that the most vicious were able to rise to the top quickly, and total war became total crime. The men of the Thirty Years War era were not more debased persons than those of the War of the Austrian Succession; the totality of the warfare brought out the totality of their nature in a way which later wars did not.

Despite all the unity movements of the 20th Century, the fact remains that the underlying issues are more sharply drawn than at any time since at least The Thirty Years War, if not far more so. It is not surprising that total war is being waged, and the responsibility for initiating it rests, according to an English scholar, with Great Britian, which, on May 11,

1940, began the total bombing of civilian centers.[10]   The War
Trials which followed were again instances, not of justice but
of total war and first demanded by Stalin as such.[11]   When
Britain and the United States went through the hypocritical
facade of a trial, Stalin apparently moved in sardonic humor
to lay bare their hypocrisy by pressing charges for the Katyn
Forest Massacre, of which he was known to be guilty, against
the Germans, to the embarrassment of the British and Americans.[12]   Prior to that, the very entry of the United States
into the war, as well as much of the warfare, was not
without its conspiracies.[13]

The U.N., by placing total power within man's grasp,
has heightened accordingly the potentialities for all total
conspiracies.   It is as a result the stage setting for a vast
inter-play of forces that use the facade of the U.N. as
camouflage for unrelenting drives to power.   At each critical
point of tension, such as Israel and Katanga, great and total
stakes are at issue below the surface of publicized events.
Total war is under way, and hence total conspiracy.

---

[10] F. J. P. Veale: *Advance to Barbarism, How the Reversion to
Barbarism in Warfare and War-Trials Menaces Our Future*, pp. 121 ff.,
126, 175 f., 262.   Appleton, Wisconsin: C. C. Nelson, 1953.   Foreword
by Rev. William Ralph Inge.

[11] *Ibid.*, pp. XI f., 140.

[12] *Ibid.*, pp. 185 ff.   See also F. J. P. Veale: *Crimes Discreetly
Veiled*, pp. 38 ff.   London: Cooper, 1958.   On Katyn, Poland, and the
Allies, see Edward J. Rozek: *Allied Wartime Diplomacy: A Pattern
in Poland;* New York: John Wiley and Sons, 1958.

[13] Charles Callan Tansill: *Back Door to War, Roosevelt's Foreign
Policy, 1933-1941;* Chicago: Regnery, 1952.   Charles A. Beard: *Presi-
dent Roosevelt and the Coming of the War, 1941;* New Haven: Yale,
1948.   George Morgenstern: *Pearl Harbor, The Story of the Secret
War;* New York: Devin-Adair, 1947.   David L. Hoggan: *Der erzun-
gene Krieg;* Tubingen.   Rear Admiral Robert A. Theobald: *The Final
Secret of Pearl Harbor, The Washington Contribution to the Japanese
Attack;* New York: Devin-Adair, 1954.   John Howland Snow: *The
Case of Tyler Kent*, New Canaan, Connecticut: Long House, (1946)
1962.   George Racey Jordan, with Richard L. Stokes: *From Major
Jordan's Diaries* (1952);   New York: Bookmailer, 1961.   Anthony
Kubek: *How the Far East Was Lost, American Policy and the Creation
of Communist China, 1941-1949;* Chicago: Regnery, 1963.   Many other
works can be cited.   In this context, the attempts to suppress revisionism
are noteworthy; see Harry Elmer Barnes: *Blasting the Historical
Blackout* (Washington: Liberty Lobby, n.d.) and *Revisionism and*

A fifth aspect of conspiracy must now be noted. The more a conspiracy is concerned with power in priority to a faith, the more unscrupulous will its activities and alliances become. It will join forces with anyone and sacrifice both friend and foe without any moral restraint in order to attain its goals. The alliance of corrupt politics with corrupt business, labor, and religion, and clearly with crime, has long been noted. In the United States, the Progressives and Muckrakers waged a major battle against this alliance.[14] Particulary important was the work of Franklin Hichborn.[15]

But the alliance with crime is not a necessary ingredient of this position which is rather the primary allegiance to power and a commensurate ruthlessness. This the various Establishments tend to show signs of possessing.[16] The activities of criminal syndicate[17] make pallid reading in comparison to the activities of Communism,[18] of Zionism, [19] of

Brainwashing, n.d. For a counter-thesis regarding the war as conspiracy, see Michael Sayers and Albert E. Kahn: *The Great Conspiracy, The Secret War Against Soviet Russia;* Boston: Little, Brown, 1946.

[14] See D. G. Phillips: *The Treason of the Senate. The Autobiography of Lincoln Steffens;* New York: Harcourt, Brace 1931. Lincoln Steffens: *The Shame of the Cities*, New York: Sagamore, 1957. Harvey Swados, ed.: *Years of Conscience, The Muckrakers, an Anthology;* Cleveland: Meridian, 1962.

[15] See Franklin Hichborn: *"The System" as Uncovered by the San Francisco Graft Prosecution*, San Francisco: Barry, 1915; see also Hichborn's four volumes on the *Story of the California Legislature, 1909, 1911, 1913, 1921*, S. F. Barry.

[16] In the U.S., Martin Dies has reported his clashes with the Establishment in *Martin Dies' Story*, New York: Bookmailer, 1963; note his comments on "Book-burning—Liberal Style," pp. 105-114, etc. On studies of the Establishment, see Dan Smoot: *The Invisible Government*, Dallas: Dan Smoot Report, 1962; Kent and Phoebe Courtney: *America's Unelected Rulers*, New Orleans: Conservative Society of America, 1962; Bryton Barron: *The Untouchable State Department*, Springfield, Virginia: Crestwood Books, 1962; Mary M. Davison: *The Secret Government of the United States*, The Greater Nebraskan, 1962. For a liberal English view of the British situation, see Hugh Thomas, ed.: *The Establishment, A Symposium*, New York: Potter, 1959.

[17] See *Organized Crime and Illicit Traffic in Narcotics, Parts 1 and 2*, Hearings before the Permanent Subcommittee on Investigations of the Committee on Government Operations, U. S. Senate, 88th Congress. Washington: Government Printing Office 1963.

[18] H.C.U.A.: *Facts on Communism, vol. II, The Soviet Union, From Lenin to Khrushchev*, Washington, 1961; Joint Committee on Atomic

the U.S. State Department,[20] the U.S. Central Intelligence Agency,[21] of foundations,[22] and many other groups, in capital, labor, religion, education, and so on. Suffice it to say that all too prevalently the lust for power becomes more and more contemptuous of moral law in its drive for control. With closer ties of communication added to international organizations, what once were village, class or national cabals are now too often international scourges.

A sixth aspect of conspiracy thus becomes apparent. The drive for power knows no limits; its rationale is to be as god, and hence it is itself law in its every wish. Total warfare, in and out of war, and total conspiracy have as their goal *total control.* This means the control of men through their minds, by means of controlled news media, schools and churches, and also control of men economically, in particular through the control of money.

There is no question that Andrew Jackson, in his "Veto Message" of July 10, 1832, believed that the Bank of the United States was a conspiracy against the people, "Unauthorized by the Constitution, subversive of the rights of the States, and dangerous to the liberties of the people." Wealthy and powerful Americans and foreigners were in league against the people behind the facade of the Bank. Jackson could tolerate no evil as necessary: "There are no necessary evils in government. Its evils exist only in its

---

Energy: *Soviet Atomic Espionage,* Washington, 1951; Senate Committee on the Judiciary: *A Communist Plot Against the Free World Police,* Washington, 1961. U. S. Senate Committee on the Judiciary: *Communist Control on Religious Activities,* 1959; etc.

[19] Tuvia Ben Sholem: *The Truth About Israel,* New York: American Israel Publishing Co., 1962; Alfred Lilienthal: *What Price Israel,* Chicago: Regnery, (1953) 1962: Richard P. Stevens: *American Zionism and U. S. Foreign Policy* (1942-1947), New York: Pageant, 1962; editorial, *The Realist,* p. 3 no. 47, February, 1964; Alfred M. Lilienthal: *There Goes The Middle East,* New York: Devin-Adair 1957; Douglas Reed *Somewhere South of Suez,* New York: Devin-Adair, 1951.

[20] Bryton Barron: *Untouchable State Department.*

[21] See Gen. Arturo Espaillat: *Trujillo: The Last Caesar,* Chicago: Regnery, 1963; Lyle C. Wilson, "New Book on Trujillo Charges Bribery," *Palo Alto,* Calif. *Times* Monday, December 9, 1963 p. 8.

[22] Rene A. Wormser: *Foundations: Their Power and Influence,* New York: Devin-Adair, 1958.

abuses."[23] The Civil War saw the banking powers working on both sides to effect a control of money, and of civil governments and people through money.[24] In the century following the Civil War, many powerful fortunes were established, and more than a few writers have ascribed great powers to them.[25] There is no lack of truth, in the main, in such studies, but the heart of the matter lies elsewhere. Industry, transportation, news and other centers of power rest today on the foundation of finance capitalism and are accordingly predominantly subservient to the financial powers. Hildreth long ago observed the source of the danger;

---

[23] See James D. Richardson: *A Compilation of the Messages and Papers of the Presidents, 1789-1902*, vol. II, pp. 576-591. Washington, 1904. See also Thomas Hart Benton: *Thirty Years' View*, vol. I, pp. 187-205. New York: Appleton, 1854. According to Gustavus Myers: *History of the Great American Fortunes* (New York: Modern Library, 1937), p. 556 n., "Under the surface, the Rothschild's long had a powerful influence in dictating American financial laws. The law records show that they were powers in the old Bank of the United States." See on the Rothschilds, Count Egon Caesar Corti: *The Rise of the House of Rothschild, 1770-1830*, and *The Reign of the House of Rothschild, 1830-1871*, New York: Cosmopolitan, 1928. The origins of the Bank of England are deserving of attention. Established in the late 17th Century on the overtures to Parliament of William Paterson (1658-1719), its major figure was Charles Montagu (1661-1715), first Earl of Halifax and originator of the English national debt. The family's 20th Century leaders include Montague Collet Norman (1871-1950) Governor of the Bank of England, 1920-1944; and the foreign secretary, 1938-40, and ambassador to the U. S., 1941-46, Edward Frederick Lindley Wood, Earl of Halifax (1881-1959) concerning whom see Hoggan: *Der erzungene Krieg*.

[24] See Myers p. 406; Carl Sandburg: *Abraham Lincoln, The Prairie Years and The War Years*, one vol. ed., p. 383, New York: Harcourt, Brace 1954; Burton J. Hendrick: *Statesmen of the Lost Cause, Jefferson Davis and His Cabinet*, pp. 182-232, New York: Literary Guild, 1939; on the desire of Chase to create a central bank, see Auguste Langel: *The United States During the Civil War*, pp. 274 ff., (1866), introduction and notes by Allan Nevins, Bloomington: Indiana University Press 1961.

[25] Ferdinand Lundberg: *America's 60 Families;* New York: Vanguard, 1938. Arthur D. Howden Smith: *Men Who Rule America, A Study of the Capitalistic System and Its Trends Based on Thirty Case Histories;* Indianapolis: Bobbs-Merrill, 1936. Emmanuel M. Josephson: *Rockefeller "Internationalist," The Man Who Misrules the World;* New York: Chedney Press, 1952. Anna Rochester: *Rulers of America, A Study of Finance Capital;* New York: International Publishers, 1936.

A bank, whether great or small, naturally and necessarily falls under the influence and control of a few individuals. If there is but one great bank, bank accommodations will be limited, for the most part, to the friends, favorites, proteges and toad-eaters of the few great capitalists who will usurp its management; and the monopoly of banking will tend necessarily to produce a monopoly of business,—for those possess a monopoly of business who enjoy a monopoly of the means necessary to carry it on.[26]

And this has happened. Through central banking, nations and people are delivered into bondage to international finance. The Federal Reserve System was created ostensibly to remedy the financial situation.[27]   Attacks had been made on "The Money Trust," and a very inadequate and faulty investigation made of it by the Pujo Committee of Congress, its results reported by Louis D. Brandeis in *Other People's Money, And How the Bankers Use It* (1913).   With the Federal Reserve Act, the very evils criticized were quickly enthroned so that it could be said, "Banking, as it is conducted today, is actually a conspiracy operating against society."[28] One notable scholar has titled his work *The Federal Reserve Conspiracy*.[29]   What is the conspiracy involved in money today?   The clue is in a statement made by Governor Marriner Eccles of the Federal Reserve Board before the House Banking and Currency Committee: "Debt is the basis for the creation of money."   Not too long before America's entry into into World War II, Eccles said, "If there were no debts in our money system, there would be no money."[30]   As far back as 1935, before the major expansion of debt money, it

[26] R. Hildreth: *Banks, Banking, and Paper Currencies*, p. 150. Boston: Whipple & Damrell, 1840.

[27] For the claims in its favor, see George D. Bushnell: *Fundamentals of Banking, How a Bank Works*, p. 22 ff. New York: American Institute of Banking, (1943) 1951.

[28] Gertrude M. Coogan: *Money Creators*, p. 118.   Introduction by Robert L. Owen.   Hawthorne, California: Omni, (1935) 1963.

[29] Eustace Mullins: *The Federal Reserve Conspiracy*, Union, New Jersey: Christian Educational Assn., 1954.   Of interest also is Ezra Pound: *Impact, Essays on Ignorance and the Decline of American Civilization*, Chicago: Regnery, 1960.   See also Eustace Mullins: *This Difficult Individual, Ezra Pound*, New York: Fleet, 1961.

[30] Mullins: *Federal Reserve Conspiracy*, pp. 78, 118, 129.

was noted "that more than 95% of all the nation's money is based upon its debt instead of its wealth."[31] This is a difficult concept for most people to realize; they are used to thinking of money as wealth, not as a permanent debt, if not an outright sale into slavery of their country and its future into the hands of money-lenders. The Federal Reserve System is a money trust, privately owned, over which the Federal Union has little control. The Federal Reserve System issues paper money which the United States of America, on the face thereof, guarantees, not the Federal Reserve itself. When the U.S. needs money, it issues bonds for the needed amount to the Federal Reserve System, which then issues to the U.S. Government the equivalent amount in new currency printed by the U.S. Bureau of Engraving and Printing. At no cost to itself, the Federal System issues or creates money against which the people must pay interest on bonds, and every expansion of currency is an expansion of debt. On the other hand, when the Federal Reserve System wants new currency, it simply calls for it from the Bureau of Engraving and secures it, debt-free. This fantastic system, common to most nations, is a form of slavery without manumission. Few protests have been made against the Federal Reserve System by persons in power, and such protests have been peripheral to the main issue.[32]

Let us examine some of the implications of Eccles' statements, i.e., "Debt is the basis for the creation of money. . .If there were no debts in our money system, there would be no money." When the U.S. federal government wants money, a hundred million dollars, for example, it prints and turns over interest-bearing bonds for that amount to the federal reserve system, which then creates money by simply asking the U.S. Bureau of Engraving to print up a hundred million dollars. Three things are immediately created, as it were, out of nothing: first, a hundred million dollars in paper money, and, second, a debt for those interest-bearing bonds which will take *more* than that hundred million to satisfy! But, third, money, the measure and medium of wealth, now represents *not wealth but debt,* and the existence of most

---

[31] Coogan: *Money Creators,* p. 149.

[32] See for example *The Memoirs of Herbert Hoover, The Great Depression, 1929-1941,* pp. 6 ff. New York: Macmillan, 1952.

paper currency represents an almost irredeemable debt and mortgage against the entire country. *Money that is itself debt cannot retire debt,* because it represents, every day it is in existence, an increasing interest debt against the country above and beyond its face value. Although it is sometimes said, of the national debt, that "we owe it to ourselves," in actuality we owe it to the money-lenders who are in and behind the federal reserve system. Thus, although politicians may promise a balanced budget, they are likely to gain more power by increasing debt, for in a debt-free country, the citizenry is strong and the civil government is limited. In a debt-ridden country, taxes increase, liberties decrease, and the civil government, increasingly less responsive to the will of the citizenry, increases its own power over the people even as it vastly enlarges the power of the invisible government over all. All in all, it is clear that *debt is the road to total slavery,* and the Christian, both as a person and in his organized society, must recognize the truth of Scripture when it orders, "Owe no man anything, but to love one another" (Rom. 13:8).

Bad as this situation is, the Bretton Woods, 1944, agreement establishing an International Monetary Fund compounded the evil. The Fund is exempt from law and taxation by any government, national or international, and it cannot be the object of any legal proceedings without its permission.[33] The result is a money-making and money-controlling agency whose powers are steadily coming closer to total power. In 1963, it was proposed by J. R. Cuthbertson, economist of Lazard Bros. and Co., London merchant bankers, that, before the price of gold be raised, all nations transfer by bookkeeping their gold to the International Monetary Fund. "They would receive credit notes in exchange." At "zero hour," all nations would devalue their currencies in terms of gold. If gold were advanced 50%, from $35 an ounce to $52.50, "The I.M.F. would thus have an immense 50% bookkeeping profit on the transaction."[34] The nations would have, of course, a 50% loss financially and a greater loss of self-government to a

---

[33] Harry Dexter White was the chief architect of the I.M.F. His concept of it is defended by Nathan White: *Harry D. White,* pp. 254-266, 287, 307.

[34] Gaston Coblentz, " 'Without Tears' Scheme to Boost Price of Gold," in the San Francisco *Examiner,* Monday, January 7 1963.

purely private agency. The I.M.F. is a profit-making institution.[35] It binds member nations to gold and the dollar, both of which are firmly controlled, in the name of *monetary unity.*[36]

How shall we evaluate these things? It is possible, and many have done it, to begin naming the international money-lenders, some known and others unknown, who are involved at the heart of these things, but this is an exercise in futility. It has been done for more than a century, and before that in many an era, without any appreciable effect. Knowledge is important, but it is not knowledge which saves men, and the public announcement of *all* the relevant names would in no wise alter the situation in any basic respect. The issue is *theological.* In this respect, the Fish Committee Report on Communism in 1931 was moving in the right direction when it defined Communism as first of all characterized by and advocating a hatred of God and all forms of religion. Communism must be defined first of all in relationship to God; it is a religious movement, the politico-economic form of the religion of humanity. This is true of both the Marxist and Fabian branches.

Similarly, the Federal Reserve System and the I.M.F. rest on the same rejection of orthodox Christianity. The money-lenders can control, although a very small minority, when majorities are without faith and direction. Orthodox Christians were once such a minority, a threat to Rome and its eventual successor. More than the guilt of the money-lenders, which is very real, the helplessness of the Christian West is a confession of its own sin and shame. *Behind* the "Money Trust" are, first, the money-lenders, and second, politicians without faith or courage, and, third, people who will not live in terms of the biblical laws with respect to debt. As we have noted, conspiracies are present on various sides and among differing racial and religious groups, but the *basic conspiracy* is against God and His Christ, and in some degree includes us all. It includes the clergy, who will not teach the biblical facts concerning usury, and the laity, who

---

[35] See the *Bretton Woods Agreements Act Admendment*, p. 13. Hearings Before the Committee on Foreign Relations, U. S. Senate, 87th Congress, Second Session, on H.R. 10162, March 30 and April 3, 1962.

[36] See Pierre Uri: *Partnership for Progress*, pp. 10, 80ff.

often work to keep the clergy poor and in debt to make them "spiritually minded" and subservient. It includes all who sell their future to men by debt, for debt places one under man's sovereignty otherwise than God's word permits, and not in willing and godly service but as a slave. Man must be in service to man only under God.

The Biblical law concerning usury or interest and debt is, in its main points, clear-cut. Debt is only to be contracted in emergencies, and no man, family or people can mortgage its future. The maximum life of a debt was six years therefore, all debts being cancelled on the seventh or sabbatical years (Ex. 23:10 ff., Lev. 25: 1 ff. Cf. Deut. 15:6-11, 28: 12, 44). Security of certain sorts for loans could be asked of fellow-believers (Deut 24:17, 24:6; Job 24:3), but not interest (Ex. 22:25). Unbelievers, living by another law, were not to be bound by this law, and interest could be exacted from them (Lev. 25: 36, 37; Deut. 23: 19, 20.). Thus, at best, only a severely limited usury was permitted. With the Reformation, some Calvinists held to no usury under any circumstances, with others continuing to affirm a strictly limited usury.[37] Certainly, the Christian was enjoined by Paul to pay all due taxes and live debt free (Romans 13: 6-10).

A truly Christian order, therefore, means not only a severely limited order with respect to time limits on debt, but also severely restricted with respect to usury. It cannot be one of debt money and of a debt economy. Bonds must thus be seen as clearly unlawful to the orthodox Christian, and to his institutions for they involve a philosophy of debt, and of continuing debt, for bonds are not generally retired when due. Indeed, bonds are the mainstay of debt money. Some bonds are perpetual, the most conspicuous example being the British "Consols," or the British Government's 2½% Consolidated Stock, of which some $765 million including the Consol 4%'s, are in existence.[38] Bonds commonly are continued past their due date, the issuing governmental agencies rarely having the funds to retire them. In any case,

[37] See Charles H. George, "English Calvinist Opinion on Usury, 1600-1640," in *Journal of the History of Ideas*, October, 1957, vol. XVIII, no. 4, pp. 455-574.

[38] *Forbes Magazine*, May 1, 1958, p. 24, cited in Ove Nelson: *Our Legalized Monetary Swindles*, pp. 67 ff. New York: Vantage, 1960.

bonds are a central aspect of a debt economy, the mainstay of money-lenders, and a death-knell to the liberties of a people. No "Money Trust" can be destroyed merely by exposure or by knowledge of its existence. It can be rapidly destroyed as people take seriously their faith in its every aspect and submit themselves to the sovereignty of God and His word. Most "fundamentalist" Christians are thoroughly "modernist" in their radical disregard of much of Scripture, including its teaching concerning debt and usury, and in their limitation of its authority to matters of salvation and certain limited areas of personal and social morality. There is no preaching against the installment plan, bonds, debt money, long-term debts, unbiblical usury, and many related matters. For even a limited segment of evangelical Christianity to adhere to these principles would have a shattering effect on the "Money Trust." The present debt economy will sooner or later collapse, destroying with it all institutions built thereon. A new and debt-free economy must even now be inaugurated in the healthy segments of society, lest chaos follow.

The Cardinal of Chile, in *The Mystery of Freemasonry Unveiled,* cited several kinds of international orders, including the monetary powers, as the quiet powers working towards a tyrannical society. The critical issue, however, is not to be located in these international conspiracies, but in man's transgression. The results of his sin lie "crouching at the door," threatening to master him unless he masters them by his own submission to God. "If you do right, will there not be a lifting up?" (Gen. 4:7, Berkeley Version). To regard the solution as merely the identification, denunciation and punishment of the "Money Trust" is to evade the fact of the centrality of the religious issue, the requirement that man live by the whole counsel of God. Nothing can absolve man of this responsibility.

A seventh aspect of conspiracy can be briefly noted, its affinity to revolution. The fact of conspiracy rests on a sense of destiny, of inevitable progress. This destiny is not God's predestination but man's inevitable triumph: man must prevail. It is accordingly a humanistic concept, not a theological one. It is not surprising that many who believe that progress (seen as the triumph of man) is inevitable should naturally conclude that revolution will serve to expedite it, to clear obstructions to it and smooth the road of progress. Revolution thus is held to be important in smoothing the path of history by the removal of hindrances and can be socially required even when politically unnecessary. As a result, assassination is often an important factor in revolutionary conspiracies as a means to eliminating road-blocks to destiny, and virtually all assassinations have this framework of reference.

The assassination of President J. F. Kennedy had many of the earmarks of conspiracy. Indeed, there was apparently not only a conspiracy to kill him, but also to use the assassination as a means to either discredit or even purge the rightwing, and prominent personages were quick to level "wild" charges both before and after certain facts became known. Furthermore, the extensive attempt to cover up many aspects of the case seemed to have more than "security" at stake and pointed to a conspiracy to prevent a free flow of news. The truth about Lincoln's assassination is still far from known, despite an "investigation," and there is no less an attempt today to issue as little information as possible and to rewrite history by that suppression. For whatever motive done, the management of news involves playing at god and is a conspiracy against the truth and the citizenry.[39]

These, then, are some of the aspects of conspiracy. The view of history as conspiracy, however absurd to the liberal with his impersonal philosophy, is a basic aspect of the perspective of orthodox Christianity. As Psalm 2 presents it, the ungodly nations and peoples rage, they conspire together and imagine a vain thing, the triumph of their conspiracy. Precisely because it is a vain thing, the orthodox Christian's philosophy of history cannot make the conspiracy, however central to the stage of history, the main fact of history. Believing as he must in the sovereignty and predestinating power of God, the meaning of history is for him transcendental. The main fact is the eternal decree and the certainty of the Son's victory, Who shall make the nations His inheritance and possess the ends of the earth, in history

---

[39] Religious use was made of the dead Kennedy by the religion of humanity. He became a martyr, and, according to one "ballad," sung by Anthony Newley on Saturday, January 11, 1964, on a TV program, "Hollywood Palace," a messiah who died to save us all.

and beyond history. Now therefore, "act wisely; be warned O rulers of the earth" lest you perish in your way (Ps. 2:10, Berkeley Version).

This assurance of victory is the hallmark of faith. William Bradford, on writing of the Pilgrims' landing on America's shores, saw cause, in the face of all problems, for both gratitude and the assurance of victory, writing:

> What could now sustaine them but the spirite of God and his grace? May not and ought not the children of these fathers rightly say: Our fathers were Englishmen which came over this great ocean, and were ready to perish in this wilderness; but they cried unto the Lord, and he heard their voyce, and looked on their adversitie, etc. Let them therefore praise the Lord, because he is good and his mercies endure for ever. Yea, let them which have been redeemed of the Lord, shew how he hath delivered them from the hand of the oppressour. When they wandered in the deserte willderness out of the way, and found no citie to dwell in, both hungrie and thirstie, their sowle was overwhelmed in them. Let them confess before the Lord his loving kindness and his wonderful works before the sons of men.[40]

If this faith be obsolete, then its victory is obsolete also.

---

[40] William T. Davis, ed.: *Bradford's History of Plymouth Planta-tion, 1606-1646,* p. 97. New York: Scribner, 1908.

Appendix 1: Localism and the Police Power

Words, more than anything else, are easily subverted. Anyone can appropriate a word and apply it, ignorantly or willfully, in a context where a false sense is slipped in under the connotation of a standard meaning. No subverter of any calibre has ever neglected the ready tool of linguistics and semantics. A ready instance of the misuse of words is the word "republic." Its meaning is important to many American conservatives; it is the designation of the U.S. which appears, for example, in the Pledge of Allegiance. But the word "republic" has also been appropriated for a radically different meaning by the U.S.S.R. The various districts of the Soviet State are called "republics."

No less an instance of perversion is the word "police." In the strict sense of the word, many countries lack a true police, and the U.S.S.R. is one of them. Americans, accustomed to regarding the police as the agencies of law and order, automatically apply that word to foreign orders. Thus, Charles Foltz, Jr., in the U.S. News & World Report, speaks of Soviet "policemen."[1] Properly speaking, there are no police in the Soviet Union, only political agents and the military power. The arms of Soviet power are, first, the Communist Party, which, by its network of informants, controls, and powers, is important in the execution of Soviet decrees. Second, there are the so-called secret police, a state-controlled, centralized body of political agents, whose purpose is not police work but the maintenance of political power. Third, there is the military power. The army, in barracks across the country, patrols the cities with little or no know-

---

[1] "Crime and Punishment in the Soviet Union Today," *U. S. News & World Report*, p. 90 f., vol. LVI, no. 9, March 2, 1964.

ledge of police work.   These are "Bolshevism's three pillars of strength."[2]   A fourth arm, even more important, and even more unrelated to police work, is the Communist Security System, "the system of the invisible government" of the U.S.S.R.[3] The police as such do not exist in the U.S.S.R., and are an object of hatred by Communists, a target for abolition. The Communist goal is to supplant the local police with a national body of political agents.

It is important, therefore, to understand what the police are, and the nature of their functions.   The principles of police operation are often formulated.

> These are: (1) the first duty of the police is the prevention of crime; (2) efficiency is to be judged by the absence of crime rather than by the number of arrests; (3) police duties must be carried out impartially; (4) punishment is not part of the police function but belongs to the courts and correctional institutions; and (5) the effort to save lives must be made even in the face of personal danger.[4]

In this day and age, many are content to define things in terms of existing function rather than nature and meaning. To define the meaning of the police, let us examine their origin, purpose, and nature.

The word "police" comes from the Greek word *polis,* and the *polis* was the Greek city-state.   In size, it varied from a single city or port, to a city and its environs, so that it is best comparable to a modern city or country.   Police, in the true sense, are:

1.   A locally controlled and hence decentralized agency which is unrelated to other police bodies of other cities or counties and lacking in any national federation or union.[5] The police, properly, are city and county law enforcement men.

---

[2] Arnold Reifer: *Design for Terror,* p. 54. New York: Exposition, 1962.

[3] See *Congressional Record,* August 5, 1957, pp. 13,681-13, 685. Remarks of Congressman Timothy P. Sheehan, Illinois, and the Sudetendeutche Landsmannschaft document.

[4] David A. Booth, "Foreword," to Samuel G. Chapman and Col. T. Eric St. Johnston: *The Police Heritage in England and America,* p. 9. East Lansing, Michigan, Michigan State University, 1962.

[5] See Chapman and Johnston: *The Police Heritage,* p. 29 f.

2.   The police are not a military body, even if in uniform. They are civilians in every sense of the word, and their authority is a civilian authority.

3.   The police are supported by the local property owners, whose agency they are, by means of a tax on property. The entire support of the police is local, and it is the property tax.

4.   Their orientation is accordingly local, and the protection of life and property is their essential task. They are thus essentially a non-political body.

5.   The local orientation of the police means also no national responsibility. Federal law is outside the jurisdiction of the police.

6.   The police are not only supported by the local citizenry through a property tax, but their source of power and authority is by delegation without surrender from the local citizenry. Men can elect a councilman or congressman and delegate to him the right to vote on their behalf; they do not possess and do not maintain a right to vote in those bodies for themselves; it is a privilege held as a member of the electorate in the person of the representative officer. But the citizenry (originally the propertied citizenry) does not surrender its police power to the police. It is delegation without surrender. The citizenry retains the right to exercise, as needed, its police power, the right of citizen arrest. This right, of course, is under law, as is the official police arrest, in each case subject to legal fences designed to protect the right of the innocent and the orderly processes of law. *True police power is thus in the citizenry and not in the state; it is delegated, not surrendered. This is the identifying mark of a true police, and the source of its offense to a totalitarian order.*

7.   The police are an aspect of the local citizenry's self-government and of their *right of self-defense. Attempts to destroy the police by destroying their purely local nature are thus veiled attacks on the right of self-defense.*

Totalitarian orders thus have no true police, and the United States represents the finest development of the police concept.   In the U.S.S.R., there is no truly criminal law in the American sense, for law is not oriented to the defense of the citizenry from criminal activity, nor is it legal in orientation. Criminal offenses are properly offenses against the state in the U.S.S.R., for all power and all "rights' are concentrated in the hands of the state.   In England, although the police, so-called, are under some local control, they are nationally paid and all under the British Home Office.   There is thus no true police in England.   Criminal offenses, moreover, are not against persons but "against the peace of our Sovereign Lady the Queen, her crown and dignity."   Ancient Rome had no police and virtually no criminal law during much of its history, . crimes being committed by slaves in the main, masters enforced their own discipline on their slaves.[6]   Later, bread and circuses was, among other things, a substitute for the enforcement of law and order.

A slave state has no true criminal law, and no police. The slave population have no rights to be defended, and no police power, or right of self defense, to delegate.   If all are slaves of the state, there is no police power but only state power.   In a free society, the citizenry can establish a local police force, exercise their own police rights, and also create private police, patrol or detective agencies to further their right of self-defense.   In the United States, in origin and development a Protestant feudal restoration, criminal and civil law are local, county law, and a true police exists, i.e., a local force to enforce laws in defense of the citizenry.   Moreover, the citizenry have a further right, written into the U.S. Constitution in Amendment II: "A well-regulated militia being necessary to the security of a free state, the right of the people to keep and bear arms shall not be infringed." Attempts to infringe this right and other rights are linked also to the assault on the police power.

And with reason, for the local police, country and city, constitute a vast and competent civilian army in the United States, each unit responsible only to its locality and without central control.   The menace of Civil Defense is that it seeks

---

[6] Richard R. Cherry: *Lectures on the Growth of Criminal Law in Ancient Communities,* pp. 56-77; 93.   London: Macmillan, 1890.

in every area to destroy local orientations in the name of "emergency." The local police pose a problem and a threat to a Communist take-over, in that it is an army beyond the reach of the central statist powers, in the states and in Washington. Communist infiltration of the police has proved to be a failure on the whole for two main reasons. First, there is a radical conflict of perspective. The police have a local, decentralized perspective, while Communists have a collectivistic and international outlook. It is difficult for them to adjust to the purely local orientation. Second, police work is hard work, and Communists want to indoctrinate and to control, not to work.

The strategy, hence, is the abolition and destruction of the local police power in its every aspect. This is being done in several ways.

First, it is being done by insisting that we have a vast problem of crime which the police cannot cope with. This myth of the fearfulness of American criminality is unfortunately believed even by police "experts." Thus, Vollmer writes that "nowhere in the civilized world will there be found a major-crime condition as staggering in its proportions as that found in the United States."[7] Statistics, here as elsewhere, are excellent liars. The United States, with its Puritan background, has major and minor crimes on the statute books which do not exist elsewhere; it has better law enforcement, and it has better records, so that statistically its efficiency makes it look worse. Moreover, except for certain major cities, most of the country has a good record of law enforcement and of a law-abiding citizenry. Regrettably, too, there is a high record of criminality on the part of certain minority groups, who now are seeking advancement, not through Christian faith and character, but through legal impositions and privileges. Very real problems of law enforcement do exist in every sector of the population, but the problem is not a *technical* one, calling for a substitute to local law enforcement, but a moral problem, calling for a Christian renewal on the part of all the citizenry, including courts and police. The subversive strategy here is to assert that there is a problem of vast dimensions, that the local police are not

---

[7] August Vollmer: *The Police and Modern Society*, p. 1. Berkeley, California: University of California Press, 1936.

competent to cope with it, and that new, centralized agencies must be created.

Second, the subversion of the police is sought by agencies which, in the name of efficiency, would establish regional tie-ins for local civil government and for the police. The city and county managers are basically hostile to the local self-sufficiency and independence of the police. The managerial system is basically collectivist, elitist and hostile to localism. Civil Defense measures seek, in the name of emergency, to create a national control over the police; the desired controls would hamper local efficiency, but they would further totalitarian control and power.

Third, the subversion of the police is sought by attacks on police integrity. Certainly, corrupt police are a problem, but corruption is a moral problem to every area of life and is a general moral problem, not an occupational disease of the local police. A good case could be made for lower moral standards among the clergy. No group is without its moral problems. Newspaper and television writers, often leftist in orientation, have done no small injustice to the police by a systematic impugning of the police forces and systems as a whole. Collectivist psychologists and psychiatrists have added to the slander, so that the opinion is often bandied about that police mentality and criminal mentality are analogous. Such vicious slanders have in some quarters become axioms of political faith.

Fourth, to the insult of attacks on police reputation is added the injury of attacks on the police by means of provocative activity. Lawless demonstrations today are an increasing instrument of social revolution, indicating a contempt of law and of the police. Such actions may be aimed against the House Committee on Un-American Activities, or against segregation, but they are also aimed against the police, in attempts to discredit them and to make them a hated agency. The conduct of the demonstrators, whatever the professed cause, is more often an anti-police action, and the continuing use made of the demonstration, after it is history, is as an ostensible record of "police brutality." All this is simply revolutionary action, and, whatever its broader goals, the immediate goal is the discrediting of the local police. Federal, and, in some areas, state authorities, have cooperated in the

attack on police authority. Thus, the occupation by federal
marshals of the campus of the University of Mississippi on
September 30, 1962 was a revolutionary act on the part of
the U.S. Department of Justice against a local community
and its police.[8]   A similar federal action occurred after the
Kennedy assassination.   Oswald was caught, not by federal
agents, who were ostensibly in charge of security and
controlled the entrances and exits of the various buildings,
but by the local police.   Further investigation was taken
out of local hands and placed in the questionable hands of a
federal commission, headed by Earl Warren.   There were
complaints that neither Oswald no Ruby could be tried in
federal courts but had to face a local court.   There were
complaints also against the right of the citizenry to bear
arms.   Thus, an assassination by a foreign agent was used
by the federal government for an assault on the one effective
agency, the local police and the local court!

Fifth, various impediments are placed on the police.
Police Review Boards are created to establish a new authority
over the police and to break the police-citizenry relationship.
The U.S. Supreme Court, meanwhile, has been steadily curtail-
ing the police power, a local, citizen's power, while vastly
augmenting federal, collectivist power and control.   This is
not an accidental development.   An infamous example of this
was the Mallory case.   Arrested for a brutal rape, Mallory
confessed to the crime when questioned before his arraignment.   No force or pressure had been applied.   The conviction
was nonetheless thrown out by the U.S. Supreme Court (in
Mallory v. *U.S.*) by a unanimous decision on the ground that
the police had no right to question him before arraignment.
Since it was now impossible to re-try him with any hope of
conviction, a professedly guilty man went free.   The Court
showed tenderness towards the rapist, but none towards the
raped woman, and, by this decision and many, many others,
circumscribed police work with such limitations as to make

---

[8] See *A Report by the General Legislative Investigating Committee
to the Mississippi State Legislature Concerning the Occupation of the
Campus of the University of Mississippi, September 30, 1962, by the
Department of Justice of the United States.*   The Committee: Jackson,
Mississippi.   See also Earl Lively, Jr.: *The Invasion of Mississippi,*
Belmont, Mass.:   American Opinion, 1963.

their work well nigh impossible.[9]   Such impediments to police work are also to be found on the state level, to a lesser degree.   Both federal and state governments are seeking to usurp the police powers of the citizenry, of the city and of the county.

Sixth, a low pay scale is used to demoralize the police. A city or county government which underpays and understaffs its police is usually knowingly trying to corrupt them and to control them.   Politicians are ready to increase bureau and agency personnel and pay, because this means an extension of their own power, but they balk, in the name of economy, at increasing the police force and pay, because a strong and independent force is a threat to corrupt politics.   In some instances, police pay is kept so low that policemen must hold extra jobs after work, have their wives work, *or* accept graft, which means a surrender and subservience to the politicians and their cohorts.   Police pay should be high, in relationship to other local officials, so that police should be definitely the "aristocracy" of civil employees.   The issue with respect to police pay is a central one.   By making the police an area of economy and limiting their force and effectiveness, corrupt politicians thereby weaken not only the police but the citizenry and subsidize themselves in corruption and criminals in criminality.

Seventh, a major assault on the police comes, by indirection, from the mental health program.   The prevailing psychiatric theory is that crime is a sickness, not a sin.   The answer is not in law enforcement on the social level by the police, and conversion on the personal level through religious faith, but the answer is rather medical and psychological.   The police, in this perspective, must give way to social workers and psychiatrists.   An uncompromising attack on this perspective has been made by a psychiatrist, Thomas S. Szasz, *Law, Liberty and Psychiatry,* who denies the validity among other things of the "not guilty by reason of insanity" plea. The mental health program, however, is gaining ground, and a prison laboratory is currently demanded by University of

---

[9] Rosalie M. Gordon: *Nine Men Against America, The Supreme Court and Its Attack on American Liberties,* p. 139 f. New York: Devin-Adair, 1958.

California criminology, psychology, education, and sociology professors.[10]

From all of this, it is apparent that the local police power is an extension of *the citizen's right of self-defense,* and attacks on the police come from the same quarters as attacks on national military preparedness, on the right to bear arms (note the double demand, national and personal disarmament), on the liberties of the citizenry, and on the processes of criminal prosecution. Those who call for a non-local law enforcement agency and "larger territorial organization," also call for the registration of all inhabitants and a legal requirement that all carry registration cards in the name of efficiency.[11] University departments of criminology are on the whole infected with such thinking and are statist and anti-police.

An attack on the local police is an attack on the right of self-defense. When the local police are destroyed, the totalitarian state will have arrived in full force. That great civilian army of local police, and a citizenry with police powers and the right to bear arms, is thus a major target of subversive activity, assault, legislation and propaganda.

As against this, it is good to note that the police are strengthening their local roots in many areas, instructing the citizenry in police powers, creating auxiliary police and sheriff's posses, all to further the efficacy and integrity of local law and order. More needs to be done, for the alienation of people and police from one another is disastrous to both.

---

[10] Carl Irving, "Profs Seek 'Lab' Prison Near U.C.," Oakland California, *Tribune,* Sunday, March 8, 1964, p. 1.

[11] Edwin H. Sutherland: *Principles of Criminology,* p. 253. Third edition, Chicago: Lippincott, 1939.

Appendix 2: Localism, the School and the Church

Originally, the prevailing orientation of American institutions was local, irrespective of their varying structures. Thus, most if not almost all churches, whatever their doctrinal stand and their ecclesiastical structure, were local in two important aspects. First, their primary orientation was not to the nation and its concerns or to the church at large and its problems, but to the local community and its membership there, under God. The church was feudal, local in emphasis, without any loss of the sense of Christendom and with considerable gain. Second, churches having a larger ecclesiastical orientation, e.g., Presbyterian, had this with reference to spiritual authority. The property and material assets were locally controlled, and immediate and ultimate title rested in the local trustees, not in the regional or national unit. The effect of this system was early felt by the Roman Catholic Church in America, and the issue of "lay trusteeism" arose as early as 1786 in the St. Peter's Church, New York, case and continued for many years to plague the church in various areas. The demand of Roman Catholic parishes to own their property and call their own pastors was attacked as an American or Protestant heresy or influence. In a sense, it was such an influence, but the irony of the situation was that this was in essence a development of an early medieval and Catholic heritage, a Protestant restoration of feudalism.

With the Civil war, a change of radical character was instituted. In order to ensure the control of border-state churches by a pro-Union clergy, the U.S. Supreme Court backed the Presbyterian usurpation of local properties. Previously, presbyteries had no title to local properties; thereafter, a legal precedent was set for various central church agencies, including a Southern Baptist Conference, to claim title to local properties. The result was a revolution in church life and structure.

Another religious revolution was the change in ministerial training. Students previously studied under a distinguished clergyman scholar and then passed a stiff examination at the presbytery, classis, or conference. Gradually, schools or seminaries arose, first independent, then more and more under the control of the central agency of the church. The result has been a decline in the academic calibre of the training. Greek, Hebrew, and systematic theology, once the backbone of ministerial training, are increasingly absent. Most churches now no longer require Greek and Hebrew, and the validity of systematics is denied. On the other hand, training in methodology has taken an increasingly larger place in seminaries, so that a "practical" and managerial clergy is the result, but a spiritually sterile one.

In another area, a similar development has taken place. Common schools were, until the 1830s, and in many areas long thereafter, entirely locally controlled and supported, and Christian in character. With Horace Mann, state support and control became an educational fact and crusade. Normal schools were inaugurated to "improve" education and the quality of teaching. The result of teacher-training has again been the rise of methodology and the decline of educational content. A simple illustration of this is to examine the difference in a century, now that state control and teacher training have gained the day. From 1857 to at least 1865 and longer, The National Fifth Reader, for example, contained prose by such men as Edward Gibbon, Henry Fielding, Thomas de Quincy, Washington Irving, Thomas Chalmers, Sidney Smith, Charles Sumner, W. H. Prescott, T. B. Macaulay, David Hume, Thomas Carlyle, George Bancroft, Samuel Johnson, Henry Clay, T. G. Smollett, and many others. The poetry included Goldsmith, Pope, Bryant, Bryon, Shakespeare, Shelley, Edward Young, Wordsworth, Dryden, Addison, Longfellow, Milton, Poe, and many more, for 600 pages of prose and poetry. The students were given a mature introduction into the world of literature and thought.[1] This is less and less true today.

Increasingly, moreover, the local community has been divorced from the school. In some states, this has gone further than in others, and local school boards have been abolished in favor of county boards, with power drifting towards the state board. In California, there is currently a measure to abolish local boards in favor of state created districts, to be 108 in number, one for each of the 58 counties,

---

[1] Richard G. Parker and J. Madison Watson: *The National Fifth Reader*, 1857, 1865, New York: Barnes and Burr.

and 50 boards in charter cities. The move is lead by Assembly Speaker Jesse M. Unruh, Democrat, and supported by the California Manufacturers Association in the name of efficiency. It is also supported by John Geagan, business manager of Los Angeles Local 99 of the Los Angeles City and County School Employees Union.[2] Local districts have opposed this measure but have been warned by William A. Norris of Los Angeles "that if they continue to be 'provincial . . . . the solution is going to be taken out of your hands.' "[3] In other words, submit "voluntarily," or be forced to submit!

During the 1950's, consolidation of local school boards was promoted heavily and pushed to its limits. The next step now is abolition of local school boards.

The neighborhood school is itself under attack. Long an important aspect of localism and important in fostering local ties, the neighborhood school is now called guilty of segregation. Integration plans in many areas call for transporting children from one area to another in order to enforce an artificial integration and to break local ties and roots. In New York City, a school official has defended this plan, stating, "We are not doing this primarily for integration, but for better education, because we are convinced that integrated education is better education." The immediate consequence has been a marked rise in white hostility to Negroes. In various areas, white groups are taking the matter to courts with some victories. The matter will doubtless be appealed to the U.S. Supreme Court.[4]

The neighborhood school, as far as control is concerned, has long been on the retreat, with teachers' associations, teachers' colleges, state boards, and other agencies steadily diminishing the local control over the school. The attack now is thus a double one: first, against all local control, and, second, against a local constituency or attendance for the school. More than integration or "efficiency" is at stake. The ability of localism to resist revolutionary changes is at issue and under attack.

---

[2] Palo Alto, California, *Times*, Friday, March 13, 1964, p. 5.

[3] Palo Alto, California, *Times*, Saturday, March 14, 1964, p. 3.

[4] " 'Neighborhood' School System in Danger?," in *U. S. News & World Report*, vol. LVI, no. 11, March 16, 1964, pp. 48-52.

Appendix 3: Revisionism and History

Many readers of George Orwell's *1984* are under the illusion that, when Big Brother gains power, he will consolidate his total dictatorship by instituting newspeak and doublethink, by rewriting history. It is questionable whether Orwell intended to give this impression. Before any Big Brother arrives, the new religion and new history must prepare the way for him and envision him as the historical necessity. The basic premise of such historiography, already with us, is a revision of an ancient law, "Thou shalt bear false witness,— if it is for the welfare of humanity in the scientific, humanistic sense." As a result, since World War II, there has been an extensive suppression of and hostility to historical studies which seek to give an accurate report and analysis of the causes and conduct of that conflict. It is inadvisable, the liberal scholars hold, to write that which would expose the radical fallacies of their position. It is equally inadvisable, the conservative scholars often maintain, to become involved in revisionism, because, to criticize Britain, America or Russia, would suggest a neo-Nazi sympathy, It has, as one such scholar has written, "inevitable ideological implications!" In other words, the *facts* mean nothing, and "the inevitable ideological implications" mean everything! For scholars to do justice to an unpopular cause is to risk "having this sort of malodorous albatross tied around their necks." In short, *bear false witness,* by silence, consent, or writing, especially if it is intellectually respectable to do so, for to do justice to an enemy, stranger, or anyone other than yourself "must simply result in embarrassing your friends."

Harry Elmer Barnes, in two brief studies, *Blasting The Historical Blackout* and *Revisionism and Brainwashing,* has described the current historical situation. Only a few scholars have challenged it; notably, in the United States, Charles Callan Tansill, *Back Door to War,* 1952, and David Leslie Hoggan, *When Peaceful Revision Failed.* In England, A.J.P. Taylor, *The Origins of the Second World War,* and Frederick J. P. Veale, *Advance to Barbarism and Crimes Discreetly Veiled,* have been active, as have been some scholars in Europe. These men do not hold a position in common, politically, religiously, or economically. Their concern is to bear true witness to certain aspects of history; their perspectives differ, but they do share a concern for historical integrity. This the court historians lack. The court historian claims at one and the same time to be impartial, to be neutral, and also to be a champion of an ideology. This contradiction the court historian resolves by identifying history with his ideology, so that total subservience to the ideology is also true objectivism and neutralism. This identification means that the meaning of history is immanent, present in the historical process in the form of a particular cause or group. This realized meaning is the incarnation of historical process, so that standards and laws are inherent in it rather than beyond and over it. Truth and law are therefore what the cause or party, history's realized meaning, does; truth and law are thus totally or nearly total y immanent, depending on the stage or realization of meaning. Truth and law are not transcendental as Christianity asserts. The court historians, whatever the court they serve, hold in common this immanentalism. As a result, they can bear false witness and call it history, because, for them, truth is what the party does and what the cause requires. And, before Big Brother can arrive, the preachers and historians of immanentalism must do their work.

24470